ICE
BREAKERS

A KIDS' GUIDE TO
HOCKEY
AND THE
GREATEST PLAYERS
WHO CHANGED
THE GAME

TOM CARACCIOLI &
JERRY CARACCIOLI
FOREWORD BY JIM CRAIG

becker&mayer! kids

Contents

Foreword

I started playing hockey on the ponds in my hometown of Easton, Massachusetts, in the late 1960s and early '70s. To a hockey-loving kid like me growing up in the Boston suburbs, Bobby Orr was everything—one of the greatest hockey players that ever played. He and the Bruins were my heroes. That is where my dreams and the journey that led me to Lake Placid and an Olympic gold medal in 1980 began.

Anything I read or saw that had to do with Orr captivated me. In 1970, the Bruins played the St. Louis Blues in the Stanley Cup Finals. I remember it like it was yesterday. In game four, Derek Sanderson passed to Orr, who scored the Stanley Cup-winning overtime goal and went flying through the air in celebration. We watched it on TV and, immediately after, went outside and played street hockey. Every goal scored that day saw one of us flying through the air like our hero had just done.

Orr, the Bruins, and hockey as a whole inspired me. Everyone needs a vehicle for inspiration. When we read, we embark on a journey and become the person we are reading about. It gives us inspiration and allows us to use our imagination. Reading provides you with your own voice to emphasize or get excited about whatever excites you. If the book is good, you get lost in imagining what you could do and become. Reading inspires.

Ice Breakers offers a chance to learn about the players who inspired me long ago and the current players who inspire kids today—whether they watch them in person or on television or read about them in the pages of a book. The stories in these pages exhibit the successes of the players and, just as importantly, tell of the journeys they took to get to where they are today. For many it wasn't an easy road, but few things worthwhile ever really are. The journey is as important as the destination.

Through the stories of hockey heroes, I hope you find inspiration, resilience, and the courage to pursue your dreams.

Enjoy reading *Ice Breakers*.

JIM CRAIG, 1980 US Olympic hockey gold medalist

By the time we were old enough to check books out of our local library, we were obsessed with hockey. The very first books we ever read from beginning to end were stories celebrating the game's greatest legends. These stories about hockey's greatest players not only helped teach us how to read but also cultivated a deep passion for the storied history of the game and its players.

Reading those books also helped us appreciate the game that we fell in love with and were learning to play. Along with reading about the legends of the game, we watched our favorite players and teams on television. When we were growing up, the Philadelphia Flyers, known as the "Broad Street Bullies," were coming of age and we often saw them play in televised national games of the week against the New York Rangers, Montreal Canadiens, Toronto Maple Leafs, or Boston Bruins on Saturday and Sunday afternoons. Because we grew up a little more than 60 miles from the Canadian border, we also were lucky enough to watch CKWS's *Hockey Night in Canada* every Saturday night during the winter. From these broadcasts, we watched and learned about yesterday's star players who became today's Hall of Famers—the very players you will read about in these pages.

It is our hope that years from now, when you look back on your days growing up as hockey-crazed kids, you will remember this book as one that got you more interested in the game and that also ignited a passion for reading.

Authors Tom (A) and Jerry (C)
in their Peewee hockey days
when they were 12 years old.

The Original Six and the Greatest Teams

For the better part of the twentieth century, the National Hockey League (NHL) was comprised of six teams. These "Original Six" cities continue to support teams today and serve as part of the rich history and tradition of the NHL. From rookies to veterans, today's players in Montreal, Toronto, New York, Boston, Detroit, and Chicago understand the history of playing for one of the original NHL teams. And they compete with honor and pride, knowing some of the greatest players to ever play in the NHL donned the same sweaters of these great franchises.

NHL DYNASTIES

Through the years, great sports teams have been referred to as and considered "dynasties." In the NHL, there have been nine (these days, they do not happen often):

OTTAWA SENATORS
(1919–20 to 1926–27)

TORONTO MAPLE LEAFS
(1946–47 to 1950-51 and 1961–62 to 1966–67)

DETROIT RED WINGS
(1949–50 to 1954–55)

MONTREAL CANADIENS
(1955–56 to 1959–60; 1964–65 to 1968–69; and 1975–76 to 1978–79)

NEW YORK ISLANDERS
(1979–80 to 1982–83)

EDMONTON OILERS
(1983–84 to 1989–90)

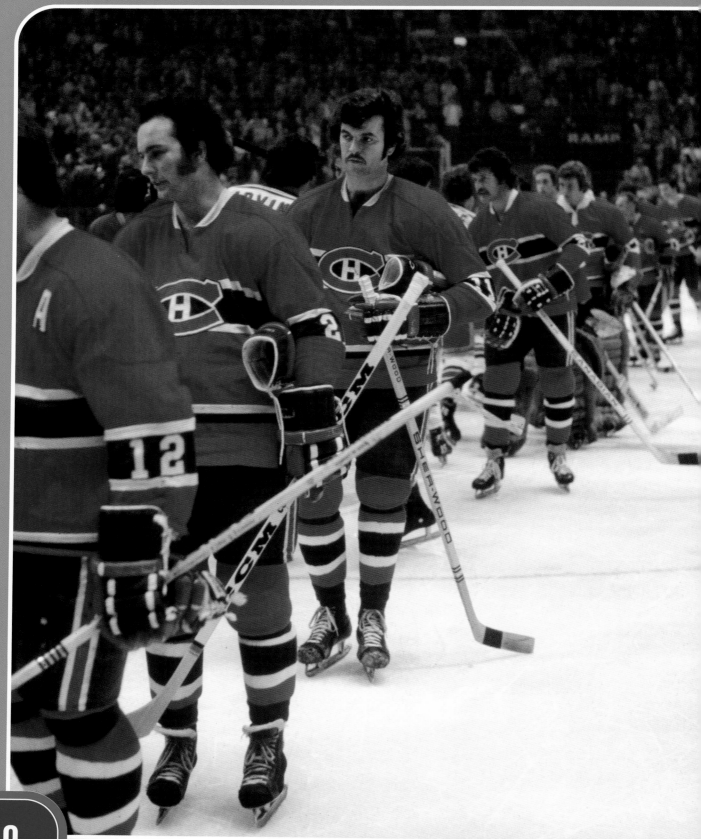

Montreal Canadiens

The Montreal Canadiens, nicknamed the Habs, have won 24 times, including a dynastic run of five consecutive years (1955–56 to 1959–60), a feat no other NHL team has matched. During that five-year run, Montreal averaged more than 40 wins a season and never trailed in a playoff series. The Canadiens also won the Stanley Cup four consecutive times twice (1964–65 to 1968–69 and 1975–76 to 1978–79). Four future Hall of Famers were members of two different dynasties of Montreal: Henri Richard, Jean Béliveau, Yvon Cournoyer, and Jacques Lemaire.

The 1976–77 Montreal Canadiens are arguably one of the greatest teams in NHL history. The team boasted nine future Hall of Famers. Opposing teams knew they would not only have to get the puck away from talented forwards Guy Lafleur, Lemaire, Cournoyer, Steve Shutt, and Bob Gainey but then also get past a line of defensemen led by Serge Savard, Larry Robinson, and Guy Lapointe. And *then* they had to beat the six-foot-three, 207-pound Canadiens goaltender, Ken Dryden.

The Habs were nearly unbeatable that season. They recorded a 60–8–12 record in the regular season and marched to a 12–2 playoff run that resulted in a parade in Montreal following their four-game sweep over Boston in the Stanley Cup Final. When the ice settled, the Montreal Canadiens had established 21 NHL records, including three that still stand today: fewest losses (8) in an 80-game season, longest home unbeaten streak (34), and best goal differential (+216).

FAST FACT:

A standard NHL hockey puck is three inches in diameter and one inch thick, and weighs between 5.5 and 6 ounces.

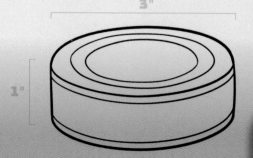

3"

1"

Toronto Maple Leafs

From 1917 to 1967, the Original Six team based in Toronto was considered one of the most successful in the first half of the twentieth century. As first Toronto and then the Toronto Arenas in 1917, the team began play in the newly formed NHL. The Arenas captured the Stanley Cup in 1918, their first of 13 in the team's history. After being sold in 1919, new owners renamed the team the Toronto St. Patricks, who would go on to win the 1922 Stanley Cup. They remained the St. Patricks until 1927, when Conn Smythe purchased the team and renamed them the Toronto Maple Leafs.

The "luck of the Irish" clearly stayed with the team as the Maple Leafs won 11 more Stanely Cups from 1932 to 1967. In the late 1940s and early 1950s, the Leafs were one of the NHL's dynasties, winning the Stanley Cup four times in five years, including three straight from 1947–49, and again in 1951, when all five games of the Stanley Cup Final were decided in overtime. The Leafs' dynasty days also included winning four Stanley Cups in six years from 1962–67, which marked their last Stanley Cup victory in 58 years. The Original Six era ended with the Leafs' victory in 1967, as the NHL expanded to 12 teams the following year.

If nothing else, today's Leafs fans are hopeful each year for another Stanley Cup, with superstar Auston Matthews leading the current team. But they also are wary of remembering their history and the years of futility in the 1970s and early 1980s with superstars like Darryl Sittler, Lanny McDonald, and Borje Salming and the late '80s and early '90s with star Wendel Clark.

WHAT'S THE WORD?

Zebra

A REFEREE, SO NAMED FOR THE BLACK-AND-WHITE STRIPES ON THEIR UNIFORMS. HOCKEY PLAYERS AND COACHES HAVE A LOVE-HATE RELATIONSHIP WITH THE GAME'S OFFICIALS, BUT ONE THING IS FOR SURE— IT IS AN UNDERAPPRECIATED JOB

New York Rangers

The New York Rangers' long and storied history as an Original Six team began in 1926, when Madison Square Garden President Tex Rickard started a new hockey franchise and brought in one of the game's greatest minds of the day, Conn Smythe, to assemble the first Rangers team. Despite leaving the team before its first game, Smythe laid the groundwork for success with players including future Hall of Famers and all-stars.

After Smythe left, hockey pioneer Lester Patrick took over as the Rangers' head coach and general manager, molding the players into a championship team. Known as the "Silver Fox," Patrick would be the franchise's face for the next two decades, helping to grow the game and create one of the most loyal and steadfast group of followers. In 1928, he led the Rangers—both from behind the bench and on the ice as a back-up goaltender in Game 2 of the Stanley Cup Final—to their first Stanley Cup. The team advanced to the Stanley Cup Final four times in their first seven years, winning the Stanley Cup twice (1928 and '33) and then again in 1940.

Throughout their history, including a 54-year Stanley Cup drought that ended in 1994, the Rangers have remained one of the NHL's most important teams. They have also showcased some of the game's marquee players at one point during their Hall of Fame careers, including Andy Bathgate, Gump Worsley, Terry Sawchuk, Jacques Plante, Bernie Geoffrion, Bobby Hull, Jean Ratelle, Rod Gilbert, Eddie Giacomin, Brad Park, Phil Esposito, Guy Lafleur, Marcel Dionne, Luc Robitaille, Henrik Lundqvist, Brian Leetch, Mark Messier, and Wayne Gretzky. After nearly 100 years, the legacy of the New York Rangers continues to grow as one of the NHL's greatest.

WHAT'S THE WORD?

Goals against average (GAA)

THE AVERAGE GOALS ALLOWED PER GAME (INCLUDING POWER-PLAY, SHORT-HANDED, AND EMPTY-NET GOALS)

Boston Bruins

When the Boston Bruins played the Montreal Canadiens on December 1, 2024, at TD Garden in Boston, it marked exactly 100 years to the day from when the franchise played their first NHL game. The Bruins, the oldest hockey team in the United States, defeated the Montreal Maroons at the Boston Arena back in 1924, 2–1.

The Bruins are best known for playing a rugged style of hockey, with a succession of generational, game-changing, Hall of Fame defensemen leading the way. In the 1920s and '30s, it was Eddie Shore who would become the Babe Ruth of hockey. With his furious fists and end-to-end rushes that resulted in goals, Shore made American fans pay attention to hockey.

In the first 15 years of the franchise's existence, the Bruins had eight first-place finishes in the league or their division, reached the Stanley Cup Final four times, and won the Stanley Cup twice (1929 and 1939). Then, in 1966, the next great era of Bruins history began with the arrival of Bobby Orr, the NHL's best rookie. In the 1969–70 season, Orr led the Bruins to their first Stanley Cup in 29 years. That year he also became the only player in NHL history to win the Conn Smythe Trophy, Art Ross Trophy, Hart Memorial Trophy, and James Norris Memorial Trophy in the same year. In 1979, Ray Bourque joined the team, playing nearly 21 seasons for Boston and continuing the great legacy of Hall of Fame defensemen by winning the James Norris Memorial Trophy five times. He retired in 2001 with the most goals (410) and points (1,579) by a defenseman in NHL history.

The Bruins' 100-year history includes six Stanley Cup championships, with the most recent victory in the 2010–11 season, captained by Zdeno Chára, who continued the Bruins' legacy of dominant defensemen.

WHAT'S THE WORD?

Shots on goal (SOG)

A SHOT THAT IS ON TARGET AND RESULTS IN EITHER A SAVE OR A GOAL

Detroit Red Wings

Along with the other Original Six teams in New York and Chicago, the expansion hockey team in Detroit also started in the 1926–27 season. Originally from Victoria, British Columbia, they were known as the Detroit Cougars, then the Falcons, and struggled in their earliest years. Fortunes changed when Montreal-born U.S. grain magnate James E. Norris bought the team in 1932. When he lived in Montreal, Norris played for a team called the Winged Wheelers. He liked the name so much he decided to call his club the Red Wings, along with creating the logo of an auto wheel with wings sprouting from it.

In 1936 and '37 the Red Wings won their first two Stanley Cups in back-to-back championships. They won their third Stanley Cup in 1943, while the mid- and late-1940s saw the addition of great young players Ted Lindsay, Gordie "Mr. Hockey" Howe, Red Kelly, and Terry Sawchuk. Sawchuk backstopped the team, while Lindsay and Howe joined Sid Abel to form the famed "Production Line," which finished one-two-three in league scoring and led the Red Wings to the Stanley Cup in 1950. The next season Howe won the first of four consecutive Art Ross Trophies as scoring champion and the dynastic Red Wings won three more Stanley Cups in 1952, '54, and '55.

In 1983, 18-year-old Steve Yzerman was drafted by the Red Wings and three years later became the youngest captain in NHL history at the time. He led the Red Wings for the next 19 years. The 1990s brought Hall of Fame coach Scotty Bowman to Detroit, as well as an influx of talented Russian players, nicknamed the "Russian Five" (Sergei Fedorov, Vladimir Konstantinov, Slava Kozlov, Viacheslav Fetisov, and Igor Larionov). Back-to-back Stanley Cup championships followed in 1997 and '98 and Detroit became known as "Hockeytown, USA." The Red Wings won the Stanley Cup two more times in 2002 and 2008 and stand as the NHL's winningest U.S. franchise with 11 Stanley Cups.

Chicago Blackhawks

The Chicago Blackhawks' journey as an NHL Original Six franchise was similar to the Rangers' in the early years. After purchasing the Western Canadian Hockey League's Portland (Oregon) Rosebuds, local coffee millionaire Major Frederic McLaughlin brought the team to Chicago for the 1926–27 NHL season. He named them the "Black Hawks" after his former World War I army division. The spelling of the team's name was changed to one-word, "Blackhawks," in 1986.

Like the Rangers, the Blackhawks had early success, with two Stanley Cup victories in their first 11 seasons (1933–34 and 1937–38). The second championship was notable because they won the Stanley Cup after posting the worst regular-season record of any team to win the title (14–25). A renaissance in Chicago in the 1960s brought Hall of Famers Bobby Hull and Stan Mikita to lead the franchise to its third Cup in 1960–61.

With the addition of Hall of Fame goaltender Tony Esposito and defenseman Keith Magnuson in 1969–70, the Blackhawks began a string of 28 consecutive years making the playoffs. But they only made the Stanley Cup Finals three times in that run—1971, 1973, and 1992—and lost each time. Future Hall of Famers Jonathan Toews and Patrick Kane joined the team in the 2007–08 season. They led Chicago to a mini-dynasty run, winning the Stanley Cup in three of six years (2010, '13, and '15). After several recent tough years, Chicago got first pick in the 2023 NHL Entry Draft and chose Connor Bedard. With Bedard, the 2024 Calder Memorial Trophy winner for Rookie of the Year, the winds of hope blow again in the Windy City.

Shorthanded

WHEN A TEAM HAS A PLAYER IN THE PENALTY BOX, THEY PLAY WITH ONE LESS PLAYER UNTIL THE PENALTY EXPIRES

New York Islanders

The New York Islanders took just eight years to go from an expansion team (1972–73) to Stanley Cup champions (1979–80) and were the first U.S. team to win four consecutive Stanley Cups.

The team's championship core started to take shape in 1972 when New York Islanders General Manager Bill Torrey picked up Billy Smith, a Los Angeles Kings goaltender, who had been left exposed in the 1972 expansion draft. Bobby Nystrom, the man who would score the overtime goal in Game 6 of the Stanley Cup Final that gave the Isles their first Stanley Cup, was chosen in the third round of the draft that year.

Torrey further built the core with crafty draft picks including Denis Potvin in 1973, Clark Gillies and Bryan Trottier in 1974, and Mike Bossy in 1977, among others. Hockey Hall of Fame coach Al Arbour was behind the bench and Torrey was the team's architect for all four Stanley Cup wins.

In 1980, Trottier won the Conn Smythe Trophy as the playoff most valuable player (MVP). The next year, Butch Goring, a veteran acquired at the trade deadline, won it. Bossy won it in 1982 and Smith in 1983. Together, the Islanders won an unprecedented 19 consecutive playoff series.

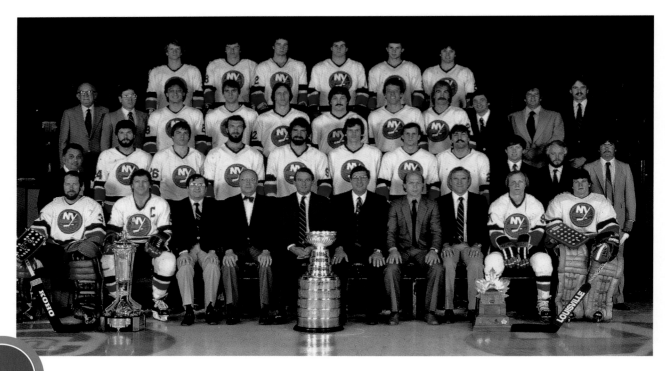

Edmonton Oilers

In 1979, the Edmonton Oilers came into the NHL from the World Hockey Association (WHA) right in the middle of two dynasties: one ending in Montreal (1976–79) and one beginning on Long Island (1980–83). Though they were like puppies at a dog park—full of energy but undisciplined—it did not take long for the upstart Oilers to form their own dynasty.

Led by young superstars Wayne Gretzky and Mark Messier, the Oilers had to learn how to win. Following the Islanders' four-game sweep of the Oilers for their fourth consecutive Stanley Cup in 1983, Gretzky and his teammates walked past the Islanders' locker room. Dreading the thought of seeing their rivals celebrating their most recent win, the young Oilers saw the exact opposite: a roomful of players tending to the bumps and bruises acquired throughout their nearly two-month march to the Stanley Cup. Lesson learned: it took hard work and sacrifice to win.

The following year, the Edmonton Oilers won 57 games, scored an NHL record 446 goals—nearly six goals per game—had three 50-goal scorers (Gretzky, 87; Glenn Anderson, 54; Jari Kurri, 52), and four players with 100 or more points on the season (Gretzky, 205; Paul Coffey, 126; Kurri, 113; Messier, 101).

When it came time for the playoffs, they took what they had learned from the previous season and defeated the Islanders by a 4–1 series margin in the final, launching Edmonton's dynasty of five Stanley Cup wins in the next seven seasons.

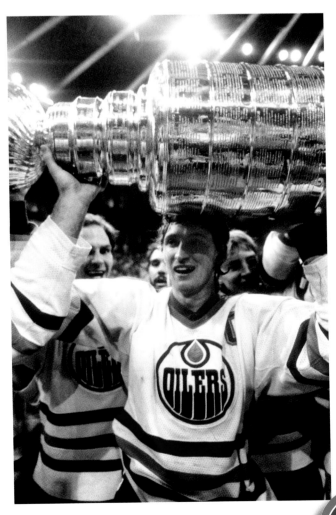

The Greatest

J ust making it to one game in the NHL is a great accomplishment. The greatest of the game reach those heights by working harder than anybody on the ice every time they step on it. No single player can win the Stanley Cup alone and it's no coincidence to see great players' names on the fabled trophy multiple times. In this chapter, you'll meet eight of hockey's greatest players: four from the first half of the twentieth century (1900–1950) and four from the second half (1951–2000).

> **You've always been 'The Great One,' but tonight you've become The Greatest.**
> — NHL Commissioner Gary Bettman to Wayne Gretzky after Gretzky's last game

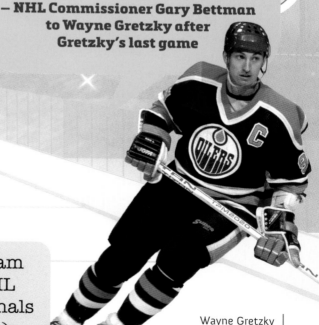

Wayne Gretzky

FAST FACT:

The 1983–84 Edmonton Oilers team averaged 5.58 goals/game, an NHL record, and had a Stanley Cup Finals record of 20-6 (.648 winning pct.) during their five Stanley Cup-winning series in seven years.

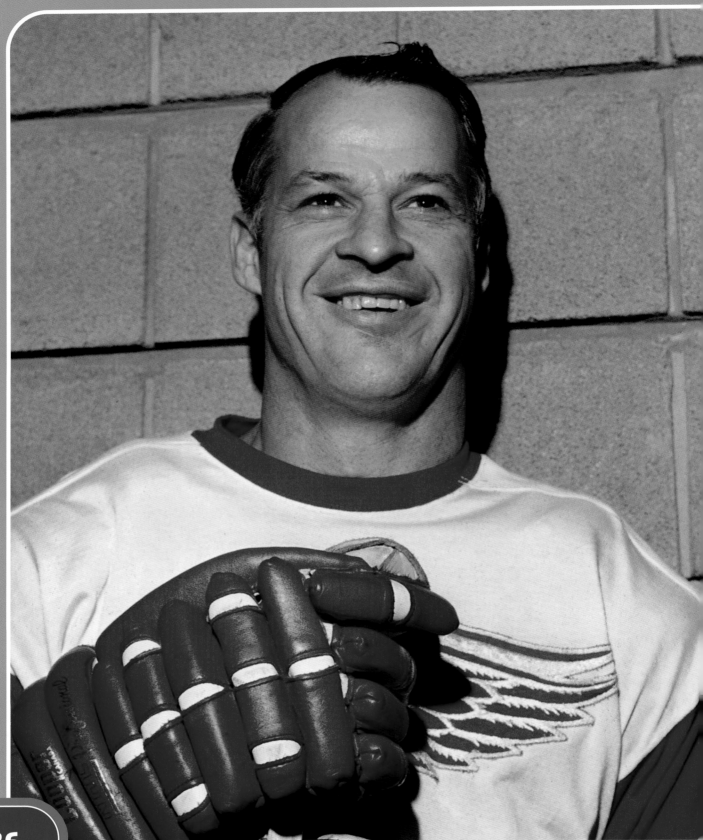

Gordie Howe

Gordie Howe grew up on the prairie farms of Western Canada near Saskatoon. In 1943, at just 15, Howe left home to attend the New York Rangers training camp in Winnipeg, Manitoba, but grew homesick and returned home. He made his NHL debut at 18 years old, as a 6-foot, 200-pound right winger for the 1946–47 Detroit Red Wings.

Howe played 26 seasons in the NHL and finished with 801 goals, 1,049 assists in 1,767 games. He was a 23-time All-Star, won six MVP awards, and hoisted the Stanley Cup four times. He added 174 more goals while playing in the WHA and ended his playing career with an unmatched total of 975 goals in 33 years.

When he was inducted into the Hockey Hall of Fame in 1972, Howe was considered one of the all-time greats. "Mr. Hockey" was lured back to professional hockey in the 1973–74 season with the promise of playing with his sons, Marty and Mark, in the upstart WHA for the Houston Aeros. Howe spent six more years playing in the WHA and even found his way back to the NHL in the 1979–80 season for the Hartford Whalers, after the WHA and NHL merged. He skated 80 games that year, recording 15 goals and 26 assists at age 52.

His last time on the ice as a professional athlete came in 1997 when, at nearly 70 years old, Howe laced up his skates for one shift with the Detroit Vipers of the International Hockey League (IHL). That made him the only professional hockey player to compete in six consecutive decades: the 1940s, '50s, '60s, '70s, '80s, and '90s.

TEAMS

- **DETROIT RED WINGS** (NHL, 1946–47 TO 1970–71)
- **HOUSTON AEROS** (WHA, 1973–74 TO 1976–77)
- **NEW ENGLAND/ HARTFORD WHALERS** (WHA/NHL, 1977–78 TO 1979–80)

POSITION

RW RIGHT WING

Gordie Howe, "Mr. Hockey"

27

Howie Morenz

Throughout his storied career, Howie Morenz was given multiple nicknames that all referred to the lightning speed he possessed on his skates. In his early years, growing up in Mitchell, Ontario, Morenz was known as the "Mitchell Meteor." As he advanced and moved through his early developmental years in Stratford, Ontario, Morenz affectionately became known as the "Stratford Streak." Upon entering the NHL with the Montreal Canadiens in 1923, he quickly became a fan favorite and was dubbed the "Canadien Comet."

Voted the most outstanding hockey player in the first half of the century by members of the hockey press in 1950, Morenz's 14-year career included three Stanley Cup victories with the Canadiens. The beloved speedster and offensive threat was the most dominant force throughout the late 1920s and early 1930s. On top of the Stanley Cup victories, Morenz would capture three Hart Memorial Trophies as the NHL's most valuable player in 1928, 1931, and 1932.

He was traded to the Chicago Black Hawks, where he spent the 1934 and '35 seasons, before heading to New York in 1935–36, where he played in the Rangers' final 19 games. Morenz returned to Montreal for the 1936–37 season and was helping lead the Habs in the regular season league standings when he suffered a broken leg against the Chicago Black Hawks on January 28, 1937. On March 8, the hockey world was stunned with the news that Morenz had passed away from complications due to his injury. In the following days, thousands of fans lined the streets outside the Montreal Forum to pay their respects to the All-Star.

Morenz was one of the first members elected when the Hockey Hall of Fame was established in 1945.

TEAMS

- **MONTREAL CANADIENS**
  (1923–34, 1936–37)
- **CHICAGO BLACK HAWKS**
  (1934–36)
- **NEW YORK RANGERS**
  (1935–36)

POSITION

C

CENTER

Howie Morenz

29

Doug Harvey

Unanimously elected to the Hockey Hall of Fame in 1973, Harvey was the most dominant defenseman of his era. Harvey joined the Montreal Canadiens in 1947–48, playing 35 games in his rookie season. The following season, he made the team from the beginning of the season and began to forge a reputation as a top-notch defender, a talented and versatile skater, an intimidator, and a force. He was a complete player that proved to be invaluable. Starting in the 1951–52 season, Harvey was selected to the NHL All-Star Team 11 consecutive years (10 times to the First Team). During that period, Harvey was also awarded the James Norris Memorial Trophy seven times as the NHL's top defenseman.

Harvey helped steer the Habs to the 1953 Stanley Cup and then to five consecutive Stanley Cup victories from 1956–60. Unfortunately, Harvey was blacklisted by the league for trying to help create a players' union during the 1960–61 season. The following season, Harvey joined the New York Rangers as a playing-coach. That season, he went on to win his then-record eighth James Norris Memorial Trophy.

Harvey played for the Rangers from 1961–64 before spending several years with minor league teams. He returned to the NHL in the 1966–67 season, playing two games for the Detroit Red Wings. The following season he joined the expansion St. Louis Blues for the playoffs and had one more shot at the Stanley Cup before falling to his old mates in Montreal. Harvey finished his playing career with the Blues, after playing 70 games in the 1968–69 season.

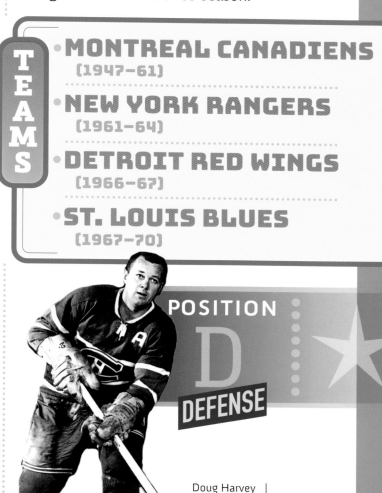

TEAMS

- **MONTREAL CANADIENS**
  (1947–61)
- **NEW YORK RANGERS**
  (1961–64)
- **DETROIT RED WINGS**
  (1966–67)
- **ST. LOUIS BLUES**
  (1967–70)

POSITION

D
DEFENSE

Doug Harvey

Terry Sawchuk

Sawchuk played half his life in the NHL, spending 21 seasons as a goalie. Retiring as one of the greatest goaltenders to ever play the game, including a then-record 103 shutouts, "tough" only begins to describe Sawchuk. When he was 12 years old, Sawchuk badly hurt his right arm playing rugby, but kept quiet about it so he could keep playing. Two years later, it was revealed that the arm had been broken and healed poorly, making his right arm two inches shorter than his right.

Undaunted, the player known as "Uke" for his Ukranian roots went on to play more games at goaltender in the NHL than any other in history. After a brief retirement during the 1956–57 season, he returned to play for the Red Wings the following season. In 1963, Sawchuk found himself on the receiving end of a Bobby Hull slap shot and decided to wear a protective facemask going forward.

Following the 1964 season, Sawchuk was acquired by Maple Leafs General Manager and Coach Punch Imlach during that season's intra-league draft that allowed teams to obtain players from other teams without a trade. Together with fellow veteran goaltender Johnny Bower, Sawchuk helped lead the Leafs to an unexpected 1967 Stanley Cup championship, the franchise's last to date. Sawchuk played in Los Angeles in 1967–68, headed back to Detroit in 1968–69, and finally played eight games with the New York Rangers before passing away unexpectedly in 1970.

In 1971, the mandatory three-year waiting period for induction into the Hockey Hall of Fame was waived and Sawchuk was added, after posting 447 career wins, including 103 shutouts in 971 games.

TEAMS

- **DETROIT RED WINGS**
  (1949–55, 1957–64, 1968–69)
- **BOSTON BRUINS**
  (1955–57)
- **TORONTO MAPLE LEAFS**
  (1964–67)
- **LOS ANGELES KINGS**
  (1967–68)
- **NEW YORK RANGERS**
  (1969–70)

POSITION
G
GOALIE

Terry Sawchuk

Wayne Gretzky

rowing up, Gretzky's dad, Walter, built an ice rink in the backyard, mostly so he did not have to take his son to the cold park every day to skate. Eventually, the strategy paid off. Ten-year-old Gretzky scored 517 points, including 378 goals as a Pee Wee. He averaged more than six points per game and helped lead his team to an overall 76–2–4 record. The young, gifted skater was garnering national attention in Canada for his on-ice exploits, including an audience with his idol Gordie Howe. The two did not know it then, but their first meeting would not be their last.

At 14, Gretzky moved to Toronto, then joined the Peterborough Petes of the Ontario Hockey League at 15 and finished his first full season the next year as the league's second leading scorer. At 17, he began his professional career as a member of the WHA's Indianapolis Racers. His rights were soon sold to the Edmonton Oilers, where he finally reached the NHL and began his celebrated career with a young group of players that would go on to create an NHL dynasty.

By the time Gretzky retired in 1999, he had won four Stanley Cups; set 61 records, including breaking records set by his idol Gordie Howe for career goals, assists, and points; won 10 Art Ross Trophies, nine Hart Memorial Trophies, two Conn Smythe Trophies, five Lady Byng Memorial Trophies for sportsmanship and gentlemanly play, and five Ted Lindsay Awards and was named the 1982 *Sports Illustrated* Sportsperson of the Year, among other accolades.

The promise of a budding hockey player nicknamed the "Great One" at a young age was fulfilled and will now forever be recognized as the greatest to ever play the game.

TEAMS

- **EDMONTON OILERS** (1979–88)
- **LOS ANGELES KINGS** (1988–96)
- **ST. LOUIS BLUES** (1996)
- **NEW YORK RANGERS** (1996–99)

POSITION

C

CENTER

Wayne Gretzky

Mario Lemieux

Mario Lemieux, a Montreal native, entered the NHL in the 1984–85 season after smashing scoring records as a member of the Laval Voisins of the Quebec Major Junior Hockey League (QMJHL). In his first NHL game, Lemieux used his six-foot-four, 210-pound frame to steal the puck from future Hall of Fame defenseman and Boston Bruins All-Star Ray Bourque and proceeded to score on the very first shot of his NHL career—introducing the league to "Le Magnifique" or "The Magnificent One."

Lemieux, who was the first overall draft pick in the 1984 NHL Entry Draft by the Pittsburgh Penguins, went on to record 43 goals and 57 assists in his rookie season. He became only the third rookie at the time to score at least 100 points and easily was named the Calder Memorial Trophy winner as the NHL's top rookie.

While Lemieux, whose name in French means "the best," had a 199-point season in 1988–89, it was not until two seasons later that his reputation as one of the greatest to play the game was solidified. He missed most of the 1990–91 regular season due to back issues but returned in time for the playoffs and led the once-hapless Penguins to back-to-back Stanley Cup championships, while also collecting two Conn Smythe Trophies.

Later in his career, Lemieux battled Hodgkins Lymphoma before retiring in 1997 at just 31 years old. He was honored with induction into the Hockey Hall of Fame and ultimately returned to the ice to help his Canadian teammates win a gold medal at the 2002 Salt Lake City Olympic Winter Games. He also became the Penguins' new majority owner, continuing to play in the dual role of owner/player until his second retirement in 2006.

TEAM

- **PITTSBURGH PENGUINS**
  (1984–97, 2000–06)

POSITION

C
CENTER

Mario Lemieux

Bobby Orr

Flying three feet over the ice with arms raised after scoring the Stanley Cup-winning overtime goal for the Boston Bruins in 1970, Orr looked like Superman. And he was.

Orr was a dynamic player from the time he was growing up in Parry Sound, Ontario. While he had skill and talent, though, the 14-year-old Orr did not have the one thing that would make him a future star: size. Still, the Boston Bruins gambled that the five-foot-six, 135-pound defenseman would grow and arranged to have him play for the Oshawa Generals. Orr continued to live at home as he played for the Generals and ended the year as an Ontario Hockey League Second Team All-Star defenseman. The next year, when he moved full-time to Oshawa to play and attend high school, Orr had grown three inches and added 25 pounds to his frame. By the time Orr was 17 and finished with his junior career, he was a solid six feet and 200 pounds. The Bruins' gamble paid off.

As an 18-year-old rookie, Orr went on to win the Calder Memorial Trophy as the NHL's Rookie of the Year and was named a Second Team All-Star. He finished second in the league in scoring defensemen and proved he could defend himself in the rough and tumble NHL. Orr had the ability and talent to take over a game with daring rushes that produced offense never seen before. He won the James Norris Memorial Trophy as the NHL's best defensemen a record eight consecutive years. He added the Hart Memorial Trophy as league MVP in three consecutive seasons and the Art Ross Trophy as the league's leading scorer three times and was awarded the Conn Smythe Trophy as playoff MVP twice. Orr was inducted into the Hockey Hall of Fame in 1979.

TEAMS

- **BOSTON BRUINS** (1966–76)
- **CHICAGO BLACKHAWKS** (1976–79)

POSITION

D
DEFENSE

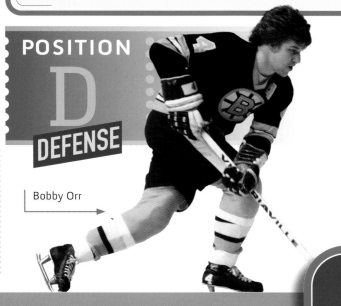

Bobby Orr

Martin Brodeur

At one point in his life, Brodeur was not even the best goaltender in his family. That distinction belonged to his father, Denis, who helped the 1956 Canadian Olympic Team win a bronze medal at the VII Olympic Winter Games in Cortina d'Ampezzo, Italy. However, attendance at legendary Soviet goaltender Vladislav Tretiak's goalie camp helped Brodeur polish his skills, to the point where the New Jersey Devils made him their first pick, 20th overall, in the 1990 NHL Entry Draft. Brodeur won the Calder Memorial Trophy as the NHL's Rookie of the Year, then added a Stanley Cup championship ring the next year, when the Devils won their first title in franchise history. (Brodeur eventually won two more Stanley Cups and two Olympic gold medals, among other awards and honors.)

During his career, Brodeur set NHL records for regular-season wins (691), shutouts (125), and games played (1,266). He won 30 or more games in 12 consecutive seasons, had 40-plus win seasons eight times, was tops in minutes played (74,438:20), tied for most wins in a season (48, 2006–07), first in playoff shutouts (25) and second in playoff wins (113) and games played (205). To top it off, Brodeur also scored three goals (one in the playoffs) and added 45 assists (third all-time) and was so unusually adroit handling the puck that the NHL created the Trapezoid Rule in 2006, which aimed to limit the area in which a goalie could handle the puck behind the net. It is often referred to as the "Brodeur Rule." He easily gained entrance into the Hockey Hall of Fame in 2018.

TEAMS

- **NEW JERSEY DEVILS**
  (1992–2014)
- **ST. LOUIS BLUES**
  (2014–15)

POSITION

G
GOALIE

Martin Brodeur

Mike "Doc" Emrick

Just how did a kid from small-town basketball-crazed La Fontaine, Indiana, go on to become America's Voice of the NHL? On December 10, 1960, 14-year-old Mike Emrick went to the Fort Wayne Allen County War Memorial Coliseum to watch the Fort Wayne Komets play the Muskegon Zephyrs, and it was love at first sight. After completing multiple degrees, including a PhD from Bowling Green University, Emrick called 47 years of professional hockey, including 40 in the NHL. He started in the International Hockey League (IHL and American Hockey League (AHL) in 1973, then went to the NHL with the Philadelphia Flyers, then the New Jersey Devils, and then national broadcasters including ESPN, TNT, CBS, FOX, NBC, and NBCSN. Before retiring in 2020, he called 3,750 games, 22 Stanley Cup Finals, 45 Stanley Cup Playoff Game 7s, 19 Outdoor Winter Classics, 14 NHL All-Star Games, and six Winter Olympics. He was inducted into seven Halls of Fame, including the Hockey Hall of Fame in 2008 as the Foster Hewitt Memorial Award recipient and the U.S. Hockey Hall of Fame in 2011 as its first media member.

Danny Gallivan

Gallivan became the "Voice of the Montreal Canadiens" and was associated with the team as much as any player from 1952–84. After an arm injury cut short a promising pitching career in 1938, Gallivan broadcast his first hockey game for his alma mater St. Francis Xavier's campus radio station in 1943.

The rest is history. Gallivan was renowned for his creative play-by-play descriptions, with "Gallivanisms" becoming a treasured part of *Hockey Night in Canada* broadcasts and folklore. During his famed career, Gallivan called 1,900 NHL games on TV and radio, including 16 Stanley Cup victories by the Canadiens. He was inducted into the Hockey Hall of Fame as the Foster Hewitt Memorial Award recipient (1984), Canadian Sports Hall of Fame (1989), Canadian Association of Broadcasters Hall of Fame (1991), and Nova Scotia Hall of Fame (1980). He retired after the 1984 NHL Playoffs.

WHAT'S THE WORD?

Natural Hat Trick

WHEN A PLAYER SCORES THREE CONSECUTIVE GOALS IN A GAME WITHOUT BEING INTERRUPTED BY ANY OTHER PLAYERS' GOALS.

CHAPTER 3

Current Stars

Each era's stars possess traits that make them stand out. In the early days of the game, players hit the ice with no helmets, less equipment and a rugged persona of being the toughest. Despite noticeable changes in today's game, the stars of yesteryear and current stars have one thing in common—they could all skate, shoot, pass, and score with an unquenchable thirst to win. Today's current stars are some of the biggest, strongest, fastest, and most-skilled players to ever play in the NHL.

> **This is really a new NHL and it is built on speed and young guys.**
>
> **—Pittsburgh Penguins owner and Hall of Famer Mario Lemieux**

Mario Lemieux ↑

FAST FACT:

To date, eight American players have been selected first overall in an NHL Draft. The most recent player to be taken first overall was Jack Hughes, when the New Jersey Devils called his name first at the 2019 NHL Draft.

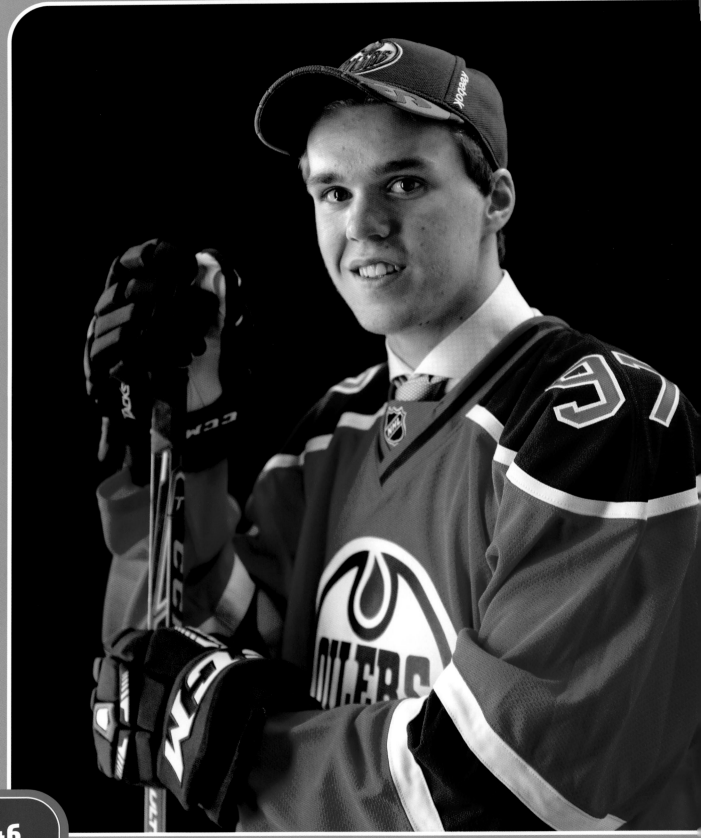

Connor McDavid

Upon leaving a record-breaking career in the Ontario Hockey League, in which he was the most decorated player in the history of the league, it was inevitable the Edmonton Oilers would select McDavid first overall with their 2015 draft pick. Since that day, the pressure to return that team to its Stanley Cup glory days has fallen squarely on the young star. Though he has yet to hoist the Stanley Cup, the 28-year-old has not disappointed the Oilers or their fans.

Through nine seasons, McDavid has recorded an average of 109 points per season and has been one of the most dominating players in the NHL since his arrival. The 2023–24 season saw him record 100 assists, making him one of just five players in the history of the game—following Hall of Fame superstars Wayne Gretzky, Bobby Orr, and Mario Lemieux, as well as current and fellow NHLer Nikita Kucherov—to reach that single season mark. In November 2021, McDavid recorded his 600th point in the 421st game of his career. He is one of only 22 NHL players and three Edmonton Oilers to score at least 60 goals in season when he scored 64 in the 2022–23 season.

McDavid also has collected the Conn Smythe Trophy for his record-setting play in the 2023–24 playoffs, five Art Ross Trophies for leading the league in scoring, three Hart Memorial Trophies as the NHL's regular-season MVP, one Maurice "Rocket" Richard Trophy for most goals, and two Ted Lindsay Awards for Most Outstanding Player (as voted by his NHL peers).

TEAM

- **EDMONTON OILERS**
  (2015–PRESENT)

POSITION

C
CENTER

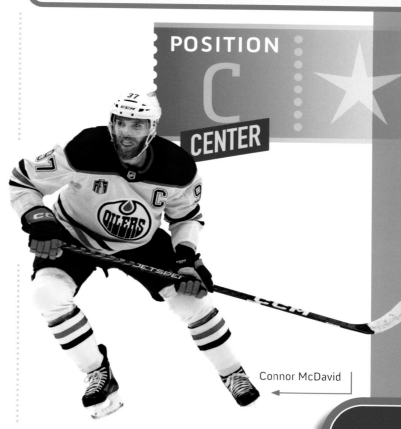

Connor McDavid

47

Auston Matthews

The Toronto Maple Leafs last won the Stanley Cup 30 years before Auston Matthews was born. Can Matthews, the first overall pick in the 2016 NHL Entry Draft, change that?

The ascension of Auston Matthews—a San Ramon, California, native by way of Scottsdale, Arizona—and other Sun Belt players like him is a direct result of Wayne Gretzky's migration from north of the border to Los Angeles in 1988. Despite success on the baseball field, Matthews gravitated toward hockey.

Like many young athletes with a "can't miss" label, Matthews' promise was identified early in his teen years. He played with the USA Hockey National Development team in 2014–15, setting the U.S. National Under-18 Team records for goals (55) and points (117) in a single season. Matthews followed this with a one-year stint playing in the Swiss pro league's National League A as an 18-year-old.

Leafs fans got excited during Matthews' rookie season when he opened the 2016–17 season with a record-setting debut performance on October 13. The young center scored four goals in his first game and was easily voted the Calder Memorial Trophy winner as the NHL's Rookie of the Year that season. The prolific sniper has already recorded two seasons of 60 or more goals, including 69 goals in the 2023–24 season, becoming only the ninth player in NHL history to record at least two seasons of 60 or more goals. Through his eight seasons, he has averaged 46 goals per season, a pace that could place him among the greatest goal scorers ever, depending on how long he plays.

TEAM

- **TORONTO MAPLE LEAFS**
  (2015–PRESENT)

POSITION

C
CENTER

Auston Matthews

Sidney Crosby
"Sid the Kid"

PITTSBURGH PENGUINS (2005–PRESENT)

POSITION C CENTER

Connor Bedard

CHICAGO BLACKHAWKS (2023–PRESENT)

POSITION C CENTER

Entering the 2024–25 season, Crosby is in the Top 10 on the NHL's all-time scoring list. The names preceding him are all in the Hall of Fame. Three years after Crosby retires, the three-time Stanley Cup champion, two-time Conn Smythe Trophy winner, three-time Ted Lindsay Award winner, two-time Hart Memorial Trophy winner, two-time Art Ross Trophy winner, two-time Maurice "Rocket" Richard Trophy winner, one-time Mark Messier NHL Leadership Award winner, and two-time Olympic gold medalist (having helped Canada to victory in 2010 and 2014) will join the rest of the Top 10 players in Toronto's Hockey Hall of Fame.

Bedard was a fresh-faced 17-year-old from North Vancouver, British Columbia, when he was picked No. 1 in the 2023 NHL Entry Draft by the Chicago Blackhawks, just days before his eighteenth birthday. Fans in Chicago immediately accepted him, and more than $5.2 million of season tickets for the Blackhawks were sold in 12 hours. Bedard did not disappoint, as he led all rookies in scoring that season, with 22 goals, 39 assists and 61 points despite missing 14 games. He was named the 2023–24 NHL Rookie of the Year and received the Calder Memorial Trophy.

Cale Makar

COLORADO AVALANCHE
(2019–PRESENT)

POSITION
D
DEFENSE

Nathan MacKinnon

COLORADO AVALANCHE
(2013–PRESENT)

POSITION
C
CENTER

Colorado Avalanche defenseman Makar arrived in Denver for the 2019 postseason just days after leading his University of Massachusetts Minutemen to the National Collegiate Athletic Association (NCAA) title and being honored with the Hobey Baker Award as the nation's top men's collegiate hockey player. The following season, he was awarded the 2020 Calder Memorial Trophy as the NHL's Rookie of the Year, and in 2022 he ended his season skating the Stanley Cup around the ice and accepting the Conn Smythe Trophy as the Stanley Cup playoffs MVP. That season he also set the Avalanche (formerly the Quebec Nordiques) record for goals by a defenseman (28) and for points (86).

Skating at full speed with agility and power, MacKinnon is an intimidating force who epitomizes the modern-day power forward. He has played 12 seasons in the NHL and may someday be regarded as one of the all-time great power forwards. Hailing from the same hometown as Crosby, MacKinnon has earned such NHL accolades as a Stanley Cup ring (2022), a Calder Memorial Trophy (2014) as Rookie of the Year, and the Lady Byng Memorial Trophy (2020) for sportsmanship and gentlemanly conduct.

WHAT'S THE WORD?

Flow, Lettuce, Salad

TERMS USED TO DESCRIBE
A PLAYER'S HAIR.

Coaches

A great coach motivates their players to compete with enthusiasm, vision, and desire. Coaches become great because they are good communicators and, often, even better listeners. Although not always liked, most great coaches understand the importance of reaching performance goals (doing everything in your power to play to the best of your ability) and not only outcome goals (winning and losing).

> *I slept like a baby. Every two hours, I woke up and cried.*
>
> **—former Washington Capitals, Winnipeg Jets, and New Jersey Devils Head Coach Tom McVie on the pressure of the job behind an NHL bench**

Tom McVie

FAST FACT:

In 1972, legendary U.S. Olympic Hockey head coach Herb Brooks stepped away from participating in his third Olympics as a member of the silver medal-winning U.S. team in Sapporo, Japan, to become the head coach of the University of Minnesota men's ice hockey team, where he would lead the Golden Gophers to three NCAA Championships.

54

Scotty Bowman

In February 2002, Detroit Red Wings Hall of Fame head coach Bowman quietly made a decision regarding his career: he was going to retire from coaching at the end of the Wings' 2002 playoff run.

Four months later, as his Detroit Red Wings team celebrated their tenth Stanley Cup victory, another poignant decision by their head coach played out on the ice of Detroit's Joe Louis Arena. Amongst the handshakes and hugs, Bowman slipped back into his locker room and laced up his skates. He returned to the ice, took hold of the prized chalice, and skated it around the ice in triumphant victory, before telling his players he was retiring.

Bowman began his head coaching career with the expansion St. Louis Blues and promptly led his first three squads to the Stanley Cup Finals. Two years later, he was behind the bench of the historic Montreal Canadiens. He spent the next eight seasons with the team, leading the "bleu, blanc, et rouge" to five Stanley Cup victories.

Bowman next landed in Buffalo as the head coach and general manager of the Sabres franchise, which had found success in the mid-1970s. Unfortunately, his efforts did not result in any championships. From Buffalo he made his way to Pittsburgh, capturing one more Stanley Cup before finding a seat at the helm of a young Detroit Red Wings team in 1993–94. He won two more Stanley Cup rings in his final nine seasons in the Motor City.

Bowman ended his record-setting coaching career having led three different teams to Stanley Cup victories (Montreal, Pittsburgh, and Detroit) and winning 1,244 games with a .654 winning percentage in the regular season. He added 353 more games behind the bench in the playoffs and won 223 for a .632 winning percentage in Stanley Cup playoffs competition. He was also honored twice with the Jack Adams Award as the NHL's Coach of the Year (1977 and 1996).

TEAMS

- **ST. LOUIS BLUES** (1967–71)
- **MONTREAL CANADIENS** (1971–79)
- **BUFFALO SABRES** (1979–87)
- **PITTSBURGH PENGUINS** (1991–93)
- **DETROIT RED WINGS** (1993–2002)

Peter Laviolette

Current New York Rangers head coach Laviolette is No. 8 on the list of all-time winningest head coaches in NHL history and No. 1 among U.S.-born head coaches. The Franklin, Massachusetts native has been behind an NHL bench for 22 seasons, including winning the Stanley Cup with the Carolina Hurricanes in 2006. He has guided three teams to the Stanley Cup Finals (Carolina, Philadelphia and Nashville), only the fourth head coach in NHL history to do so.

While playing defense at Division III Westfield State College in Massachusetts, he was also captain during his sophomore, junior, and senior seasons. He played on the 1988 U.S. Olympic team and was named captain of the 1994 U.S. Olympic team. During his professional career, he spent time in Providence as part of the Boston Bruins' top minor league team and captained the "Baby Bs" to the 1988–89 Calder Cup as playoff champions of the AHL.

His career took a turn when he served as a player-assistant coach in 1997 in Providence. In 1997–98, he got head-coaching experience in Wheeling, West Virginia, and then took a two-year apprenticeship in Providence as head coach of the Bruins, where he led his former team to the 1998–99 Calder Cup championship.

In 2000–01, Laviolette began his coaching career in the NHL as an assistant coach with the Boston Bruins. His first head-coaching job was with the Islanders in 2001, and he also served as head coach of the 2006 U.S. Olympic Men's Hockey Team in Turin, Italy. Eventually, he found his way back to New York as the head coach of the "Broadway Blueshirts," helping guide the Rangers to the Presidents' Trophy as the top team in the regular season with a 55-win season in 2023–24.

TEAMS

- **NEW YORK ISLANDERS** (2001–03)
- **CAROLINA HURRICANES** (2003–09)
- **PHILADELPHIA FLYERS** (2009–14)
- **NASHVILLE PREDATORS** (2014–20)
- **WASHINGTON CAPITALS** (2020–23)
- **NEW YORK RANGERS** (2023–PRESENT)

Herb Brooks

U.S. OLYMPIC HOCKEY HEAD COACH
(1980, 2002)
UNIVERSITY OF MINNESOTA (1972–79)
NEW YORK RANGERS (1981–85)
ST. CLOUD STATE UNIVERSITY (1986–87)
MINNESOTA NORTH STARS (1987–88)
NEW JERSEY DEVILS (1992–93)
PITTSBURGH PENGUINS (1999–2000)
FRANCE OLYMPIC HOCKEY TEAM (2002)

For one night, on February 22, 1980, U.S. Olympic Hockey head coach Brooks asked his young team of college-aged players to *believe* they were the best team in the world when they stepped on the ice against the Soviet Union at the 1980 Olympic Winter Games. Miraculously, his team believed, and they proved it against the heavily favored Union of Soviet Socialist Republics (USSR). Brooks will forever be remembered as the mastermind of the 1980 "Miracle on Ice" gold medal victory in Lake Placid. Brooks went on to coach in the NHL (New York Rangers, Pittsburgh Penguins, New Jersey Devils, and Minnesota North Stars), as well as in college (St. Cloud State University) and at the 1998 and 2002 Olympic Winter Games (for France and the U.S., respectively).

Anatoly Tarasov

SOVIET UNION OLYMPIC HOCKEY TEAM
(1960, 1964, 1968, 1972)

"The Father of Russian Ice Hockey" and "The Caviar Diplomat" are just two nicknames that described Soviet Union Ice Hockey Federation legend Tarasov. The start of Russian dominance in international ice hockey can be directly traced back to Tarasov. The game he taught on ice was often described in balletic terms, rather than rugged language. Tarasov's Olympic and World Championship gold medal-winning teams were characterized as "silky" and "smooth," their moves compared to "dancing on ice." Tarasov put his teams through rough workouts of repetitive drilling on and off the ice, but the work paid off with multiple Olympic and World Championship victories. Tarasov was inducted into the Hockey Hall of Fame in Toronto in 1974.

Jon Cooper

Cooper is the longest-tenured head coach in the NHL to date (525 wins, 279 losses, 75 ties in 879 games) and has coached the Tampa Bay Lightning to two Stanley Cup victories. In an era of parity in the NHL, when every team is as good as every other team, Cooper's Tampa Bay team is the closest thing to a recent dynasty having won back-to-back Stanley Cups in 2020 and 2021, while losing in the finals in an attempt to "three-peat" in 2022. Educated as a lawyer, Cooper started his coaching career as a high school coach in East Lansing, Michigan. His ability to communicate with his players—thanks to his legal training—helped springboard him to success at the highest levels of the sport.

Hector "Toe" Blake

Blake began his career in the NHL as an all-star and a Stanley Cup and Hart Memorial Trophy winner for the Montreal Maroons and Canadiens. He ended it as the fedora-and-suit-wearing head coach of the same organization following his playing days. Viewed as a serious, no-nonsense, pug-faced head coach, it seemed that Blake was only happy when his Canadiens were drinking champagne from the Stanley Cup. Thankfully, Blake found lots to be happy about, guiding the Canadiens to eight Stanley Cup victories in his 13-year tenure behind the bench.

Games played (GP)

THE NUMBER OF GAMES A PLAYER PARTICIPATES IN DURING THE REGULAR SEASON

Goal Scorers

Like home run hitters in baseball, goal scorers in hockey make headlines. Not always the biggest or strongest players on the ice, goal scorers just have a knack for finding the back of the net. Some of the greatest goal scorers of the game were hardly the biggest players on the ice in terms of their size. But when it came time to make the play and help their teams in crucial moments of games and playoffs, these gifted players found ways to get the puck into the net.

> **"** *He was born to score goals.* **"**
>
> **—New York Islanders goalie Glenn "Chico" Resch on Hall of Fame teammate Mike Bossy**

Mike Bossey

FAST FACT:

Former Toronto Maple Leafs captain and Hall of Famer Darryl Sittler was a seven-time NHL All-Star and scored more than 1,100 points in 1,096 games. He set several NHL records, including the record for most points scored in a single game (10 points; six goals and four assists) and most assists in a single game (7).

Maurice "Rocket" Richard

When the NHL's Board of Governors elects to name a postseason award in a player's honor, you know that player was special. The Maurice "Rocket" Richard Trophy is awarded to the NHL's top goal scorer in the regular season.

A fiery competitor who led the NHL five times in goals scored. Richard also ended his career with 1,285 penalty minutes. He helped lead his Canadiens to eight Stanley Cup titles during his career, including five consecutive Cup wins from 1956–60. The "Rocket" was the first player in the history of the game to score 50 goals in a season and compile 500 goals in a career. His first 50-goal season came in 1944–45 when he accomplished the feat in 50 games. It was a mark that stood unmatched for 36 years.

Often at his best when the game was most important or on the line, Richard held the record for most playoff overtime game-winning goals until Joe Sakic of the Colorado Avalanche beat it in the 2006 playoffs. The Rocket's final regular-season goal was scored on March 20, 1960, and capped his career total at 544. The last goal Richard ever scored in the NHL appropriately came during the 1960 Stanley Cup Finals against the Toronto Maple Leafs in Game 3 of the Habs' eventual four-game sweep. Foregoing the standard three-year waiting period for induction, Richard was ushered into the Hockey Hall of Fame in 1961.

In 1977, Richard recommended the Canadiens draft a wiry, natural goal scorer from the Laval Nationals of the QMJHL: Mike Bossy. Bossy went on to enjoy a Hall-of-Fame career with the New York Islanders where he matched Richard's 50 goals in 50 games during the 1980–81 season.

When Maurice Richard passed away in 2000, his funeral was held at historic Notre-Dame Basilica in Old Montreal, the first time an athlete had ever been accorded that honor.

TEAM

- **MONTREAL CANADIENS** (1940–60)

POSITION

RW ★
RIGHT WING

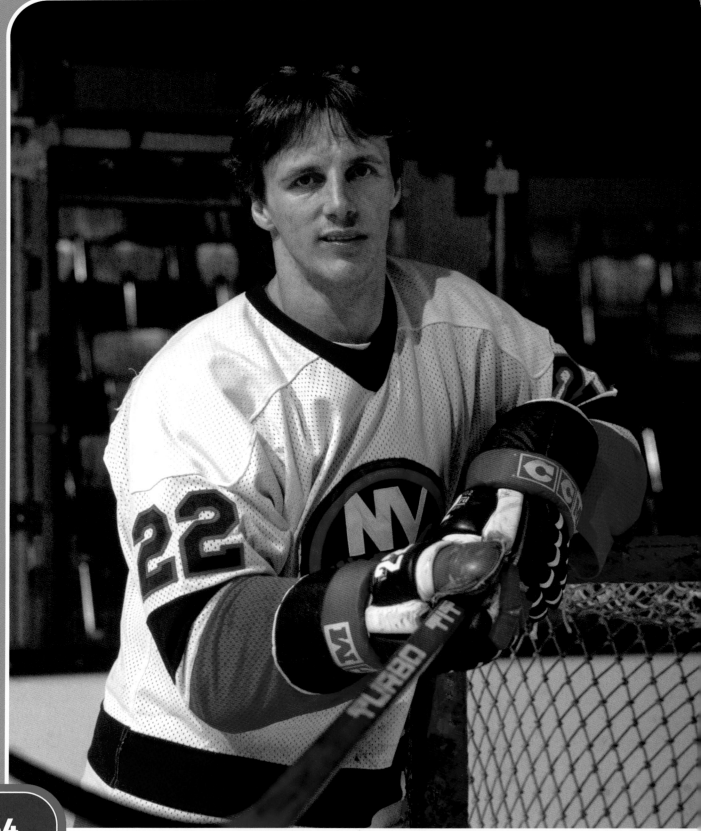

Mike Bossy

In the early 1970s, hockey in North America was seen as a tough sport. Besides having top-level skating, shooting, and scoring talent, young players also had to develop fighting skills to defend themselves.

Following a violent four years of play in the QMJHL in which he broke his nose, lost some teeth, and scored 309 goals (an average of more than 77 goals per season) while choosing not to "drop his gloves," Bossy was labeled as "timid" when NHL scouts discussed his potential. Legendary superstar Maurice Richard knew otherwise and famously advised his former Canadiens organization to draft Bossy despite the scouting reports. Twelve teams, including the New York Rangers and Toronto Maple Leafs twice, failed to draft him in the 1977 NHL Entry Draft. Finally, with the 15th selection in the first round, Bill Torrey, Al Arbour, and the New York Islanders chose Bossy and changed the course of the Islanders' history.

Despite a career cut short after just 10 years because of debilitating back pain, Bossy helped lead the Islanders to four consecutive Stanley Cups from 1980–83. He also proved himself as one of the most prolific and deadly snipers the game has ever seen. In his Calder Memorial Trophy-winning rookie season, Bossy scored 53 goals and finished his debut season with 92 points. He went on to score at least 50 goals in his next eight consecutive seasons.

Before the 1980–81 season, Bossy had a personal goal to score 50 goals in 50 games or less, a mark no one had matched or broken since Maurice Richard set it in 1944–45. After two periods in Game 50 of that season against the Quebec Nordiques, Bossy was stuck on 48 goals. With just under five minutes to go, he notched his 49th goal of the season. With 1:29 remaining, Bossy's teammate Bryan Trottier fed the right winger a perfect pass on the left face-off circle, and Bossy did what he did best: he shot and scored. Fifty goals in 50 games!

TEAM

- NEW YORK ISLANDERS
(1977–87)

POSITION

RW

RIGHT WING

Brett Hull
"The Golden Brett"

CALGARY FLAMES (1986–88)
ST. LOUIS BLUES (1988–98)
DALLAS STARS (1998–2001)
DETROIT RED WINGS (2001–04)
PHOENIX COYOTES (2005–06)

POSITION
RW
RIGHT WING

Throughout his 20-year career, Brett Hull was known for many things. Besides being one of the most explosive goal scorers of his era—including 1989–92 seasons with 72, 86, and 70 goals, respectively—he also possessed a wicked sense of humor. Upon beginning his first training camp with the St. Louis Blues, the two-time Stanley Cup-winning champion was given his pre-camp physical. When the trainer asked him to raise his arms to measure his reach, the future Hall of Famer, who would retire with 741 career goals, complied. When the trainer asked, "Is that as high as you can raise them?" Hull promptly replied, "Yeah, but I can do it about 60 times a year."

Alexander Ovechkin

WASHINGTON
CAPITALS
(2005–PRESENT)

POSITION
RW
RIGHT WING

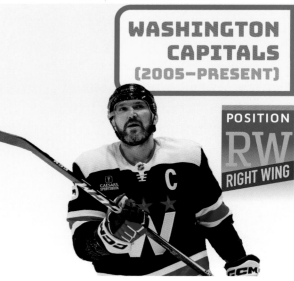

At the time of his retirement in 1999, Wayne Gretzky had scored a record 894 career goals. It was a record, like Babe Ruth's career home run mark of 715, many thought would never be broken. But following the 2023–24 NHL regular season, Ovechkin stands just 41 goals shy of breaking Gretzky's record. Assuming the 39-year-old Ovechkin stays healthy through the end of his current contract, which ends following the 2025–26 season, he will likely pass the mark that was established when he was just 14 years old, growing up and learning the sport in Russia.

Snipe

A NEARLY IMPOSSIBLE SHOT IN WHICH THE GOAL SCORER—OR "SNIPER"—SHOOTS THE PUCK THROUGH A TINY WINDOW FOR A GOAL; A SNIPER IS A PLAYER WHO CAN DO THIS ON A REGULAR BASIS.

WHAT'S THE WORD?

Jari Kurri

EDMONTON OILERS (1980–90)
LOS ANGELES KINGS (1991–95)
NEW YORK RANGERS (1995–96)
ANAHEIM DUCKS (1996–97)
COLORADO AVALANCHE (1997–98)

POSITION
RW
RIGHT WING

Considered throughout his playing career as Gretzky's "right-hand man," Kurri was more than that. It is true Kurri followed Gretzky from Edmonton to Los Angeles and then to the Rangers. But you do not get to play with Gretzky if you cannot finish what The Great One started. And Kurri could finish. During his time playing with Gretzky, Kurri collected most of his 601 career goals, helped the Oilers become a dynasty, and left the game with five Stanley Cup rings. Kurri also won the 1984–85 Lady Byng Memorial Trophy for sportsmanlike and gentlemanly play. Nicknamed the "Finnish Flash," in 2001, Kurri became the first Finnish player to be enshrined in the Hockey Hall of Fame.

Guy Lafleur

MONTREAL CANADIENS (1971–85)
NEW YORK RANGERS (1988–89)
QUEBEC NORDIQUES (1989–91)

POSITION
RW
RIGHT WING

Considered one of the NHL's most lethal goal scorers throughout the 1970s and possessing one of the game's most intimidating shots skating down the right side, Lafleur was ironically known by the demure nickname "The Flower" (la fleur, in French). The Montreal Canadiens right winger was anything but demure. He helped the Habs win five Stanley Cups while earning the 1977 Conn Smythe Trophy, plus three consecutive Art Ross Trophies and Ted Lindsay Awards (1975–78), as well as two consecutive Hart Memorial Trophies (1976, 1977). Lafleur was inducted into the Hockey Hall of Fame in 1988.

GAME SHORTHAND

Shooting percentage (SH%): the total goals scored divided by the total number of shots taken.

67

Playmakers

The nature of a playmaker is to understand the flow of the game. They must possess extraordinary vision, imagination, and creativity. Playmakers often have an uncommon ability to know where every player is (or will be) on the ice, and it is a goal scorer's job to trust their linemate to deliver the puck. While it is true goal scorers often grab the headlines, without playmakers sliding, feathering, saucering, dropping, and distributing the puck seamlessly to their linemates, there would be no headlines to grab.

> *As far as I am concerned, he is the second-best playmaking center behind Wayne Gretzky in hockey.*
>
> —Hall of Fame goal scorer Brett Hull commenting on former teammate Adam Oates

FAST FACT:

Only five players in the history of the NHL have had 100 or more assists in a season: Gretzky (in 11 seasons); Lemieux (1988–89); Orr (1970–71), McDavid (2023–24), and Kucherov (2023–24). The only other time two players had 100 or more assists in the same season was 1988–89, when Gretzky and Lemieux each had 114.

Adam Oates

Ron Francis

Upon learning the Pittsburgh Penguins had acquired Francis from the Hartford Whalers in 1991, Mario Lemieux noted, "When we traded for him in the early 1990s, he gave us an opportunity to win the Cup right away."

Francis was a "quiet superstar." He played 23 seasons, won two Stanley Cups with the Pittsburgh Penguins, and was one of the youngest team captains in NHL history when he wore the "C" for the Hartford Whalers in the 1984–85 season at the age of 21. He finished his career with 549 goals, is fifth all-time with 1,798 points, and is second behind only Wayne Gretzky on the all-time list of assist leaders, with 1,249.

Francis proved to be the "missing piece" when he was traded to the Penguins towards the end of 1990-91 regular season. The team went on to win back-to-back Stanley Cup championships after the acquisition. Francis also recorded two seasons with 100 or more points, including a career-high 119 with 92 assists in 1995–96. His years in Pittsburgh never saw him score less than 20 goals in a full season of play.

In the 1998–99 season, Francis returned to the franchise that had originally drafted him, though Hartford had moved to Raleigh, North Carolina, to become the Carolina Hurricanes. Following retirement, Francis spent eight years filling various roles for the Hurricanes, including associate coach, director of player development, personnel, and hockey operations before taking the helm as the club's general manager. Francis was inducted into the Hockey Hall of Fame in 2007. In 2019 he was named the Seattle Kraken's first-ever general manager and remains in that position today.

TEAMS

- **HARTFORD WHALERS** (1981–91)
- **PITTSBURGH PENGUINS** (1991–98)
- **CAROLINA HURRICANES** (1998–2004)
- **TORONTO MAPLE LEAFS** (2003–04)

POSITION

C

CENTER

Ray Bourque

Bourque spent nearly his entire 22-year career in the black and gold of the Boston Bruins, doing everything he could to help them win the Stanley Cup. He won the Calder Memorial Trophy as Rookie of the Year, was a five-time James Norris Memorial Trophy winner, 13-time First Team NHL All-Star, played in 19 consecutive All-Star Games, won the King Clancy Memorial Trophy for on-and-off-ice contributions to the game and the Lester Patrick Trophy, and played in two Stanley Cup Finals with the Bs. But the Cup eluded him.

In March 2000, much to fans' disbelief, Bruins' management decided to trade Bourque, their team captain, to the Colorado Avalanche. The stalwart, playmaking, offensive defenseman was welcomed in Colorado for the last 14 games of the season. Unfortunately, the talent-ridden Avs lost to the Dallas Stars in seven games in the Western Conference Final. The following year, Bourque played in 80 games in Denver, scoring seven goals while adding 52 assists. Along with superstars Joe Sakic, Peter Forsberg and Patrick Roy, the Avalanche skated to the Stanley Cup Finals in 2001.

Through 21 of the Avs' 23 games played that spring, the 40-year-old Bourque averaged 28:31 of ice-time and collected four goals and six assists. The Avs prevailed in seven games in their second round Western Conference Semi-Final against the Los Angeles Kings. They went on to defeat the St. Louis Blues in the Western Conference Final, thus earning the right to play the Eastern Conference champion New Jersey Devils for the Stanley Cup. The Avs ultimately prevailed, making Bourque's dream come true.

When team captain Sakic accepted the Stanley Cup at the end of the game, instead of being the first to raise the prized chalice, as is the tradition, he immediately turned and gave it to Bourque for the long-awaited honor.

TEAMS

- **BOSTON BRUINS**
  (1979–99)
- **COLORADO AVALANCHE**
  (1999–2001)

POSITION

D

DEFENSE

Patrick Kane

CHICAGO BLACKHAWKS
(2007–23)
NEW YORK RANGERS (2023)
DETROIT RED WINGS
(2023–PRESENT)

POSITION
RW
RIGHT WING

I t is no understatement to describe Kane as one of the greatest American-born hockey players in the history of the NHL. He left the Chicago Blackhawks in 2022 after 15 seasons in the Windy City, with three Stanley Cups and his name near the top of some of Chicago's all-time records, including points (2nd), assists (2nd), goals (3rd), and games played (3rd). He was chosen No. 1 in the 2007 NHL Entry draft and his impact was felt immediately, helping the Blackhawks start their climb toward three future Stanley Cup titles while winning the Calder Memorial Trophy as the NHL's top rookie.

Nikita Kucherov

TAMPA BAY
LIGHTNING
(2013–PRESENT)

POSITION
RW
RIGHT WING

O n the final day of the 2023-24 regular season, two-time Stanley Cup champion right wing Kucherov added his name to an impressive list when he recorded his 100th assist of the season. Before that season, only three other players in the history of the NHL had ever recorded at least 100 assists in the regular season. A few days before Kucherov became the fifth player in NHL history to record at least 100 assists in a regular season, Edmonton Oilers star Connor McDavid added his name to that same list.

WHAT'S THE WORD?

Apple

AN ASSIST.

Bryan Trottier

NEW YORK ISLANDERS
(1975-90)
PITTSBURGH PENGUINS
(1990-92, 1993-94)

POSITION
C
CENTER

Trottier was considered the best center in professional hockey in the early 1980s. He helped lead the New York Islanders to four consecutive Stanley Cups, later helped the Pittsburgh Penguins win two Stanley Cups, and retired as one of the premier playmakers of his era. In 1975–76, Trottier finished his debut season with NHL records for a rookie in assists (63) and points (95) and was awarded the Calder Memorial Trophy as the top newcomer. He went on to score 524 goals, rack up 901 assists, and record a plus/minus of +449 in 1,279 career games. Trottier was inducted into the Hockey Hall of Fame in 1997.

Adam Oates

DETROIT RED WINGS (1985-89)
ST. LOUIS BLUES (1989-92)
BOSTON BRUINS (1992-97)
WASHINGTON CAPITALS
(1997-2002)
PHILADELPHIA FLYERS
(2001-02)
ANAHEIM MIGHTY DUCKS
(2002-03)
EDMONTON OILERS
(2003-04)

POSITION
C
CENTER

At the conclusion of his 19-year career, Oates ranked as one of the greatest playmakers of all-time in the NHL. Currently, the former Rensselaer Polytechnic Institute Engineers collegiate standout and NCAA champion stands eighth on the NHL's all-time career list for assists. Playing his early career and prime with sharpshooters Brett Hull (St. Louis Blues) and Cam Neely (Boston Bruins), Oates proved himself as one of the preeminent centers and playmakers of the 1990s. He ended his career with 1,079 assists and a Hall of Fame plaque in Toronto.

GAME SHORTHAND	Average shots on goal (SOG)

Blueliners

No one position in hockey has evolved as dramatically as defensemen. Once thought of as more of a defender against the other team's offense, today's blueliners are some of the best-skating, offensively skilled, biggest, and most intimidating players on the ice. From Harvey to Orr, Potvin, Robinson, Coffey, Victor Hedman, and Makar, the "defensive position" is where these players lined up (and continue to line up) during a face-off. Defensemen no longer stay anchored from their own goal line to an opponent's blueline—sometimes they do their best defensive work by controlling the puck offensively.

> *Doug Harvey was the best defenseman I ever saw . . . If Montreal got a goal up on you and Harvey decided you were not going to score, that was it. Go take a shower, the game is over.*
>
> **—Referee Red Storey**

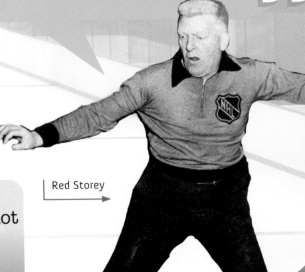

Red Storey

FAST FACT:

In 2012, Boston Bruins defenseman Zdeno Chára recorded the fastest shot ever in NHL history with a 108.8 miles per hour slapshot.

BLUELINERS

Paul Coffey

With lightning speed, a seemingly effortless skating ability, a blistering shot, offensive savvy, and bulldog tenacity, Coffey was almost the reincarnation of another freewheeling, high-flying, offensive-defenseman: Bobby Orr. Coffey played 21 seasons, collected four Stanley Cup rings (three with Edmonton in 1984, '85, and '87 and one with Pittsburgh in 1991), as well as three James Norris Memorial Trophies as the NHL's top defenseman.

The highly skilled Coffey was destined for the next level after several all-star seasons in the Ontario Major Junior Hockey League. He became the sixth overall pick (first by the Edmonton Oilers) in the 1980 NHL Entry Draft. In his sophomore season of 1981–82, Coffey led all defensemen with 89 points and was named an NHL Second Team All-Star. The following season, he tallied 29 goals and 67 assists for 96 points. In 1983–84, he finished second to teammate Wayne Gretzky in league scoring with 126 points. That season, Edmonton won their first Stanley Cup, and an Oilers dynasty had begun.

Coffey would help the Oilers win two more Stanley Cup championships before being traded to the Pittsburgh Penguins prior to the 1987–88 season. He recorded his fourth and fifth seasons of 100 or more points during his stay in Pittsburgh and helped the Pens win their first Stanley Cup in 1991. Coffey spent the rest of his career playing from coast-to-coast with the Los Angeles Kings, Detroit Red Wings, Hartford Whalers, Philadelphia Flyers, Chicago Blackhawks, Carolina Hurricanes, and Boston Bruins.

TEAMS

- EDMONTON OILERS (1980–87)
- PITTSBURGH PENGUINS (1987–92)
- LOS ANGELES KINGS (1992)
- DETROIT RED WINGS (1993–96)
- HARTFORD WHALERS (1996–97)
- PHILADELPHIA FLYERS (1996–98)
- CHICAGO BLACKHAWKS (1998)
- CAROLINA HURRICANES (1998–2000)
- BOSTON BRUINS (2000–01)

POSITION
D
DEFENSE

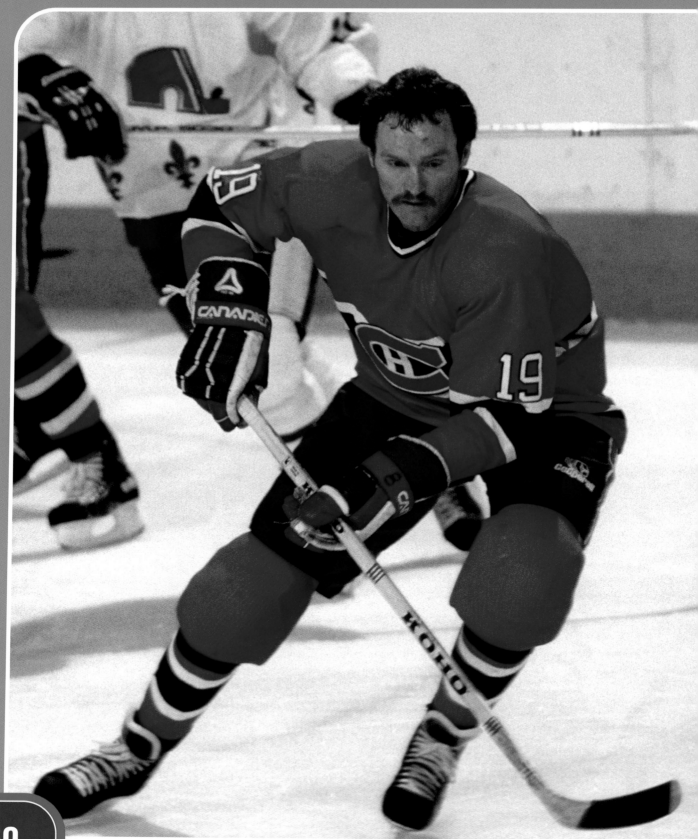

Larry Robinson

Today, it is hard to imagine that Hall of Fame defenseman Robinson was passed over three times by the Canadiens in the 1971 NHL Entry Draft. When the Habs finally chose the six-foot-four, 225-pound blueliner with their fourth pick, Robinson was the 20th overall pick in that year's draft.

As part of a defensive corps backstopped by Hall of Fame goaltender Ken Dryden, Robinson was joined on the Canadiens blueline by fellow Hall of Famers Serge Savard and Guy Lapointe. In all, nine Habs from the 1976–77 Stanley Cup team ended their careers in the Hall of Fame.

Nicknamed "Big Bird" after the *Sesame Street* character, Robinson was an imposing defender partly because of his height, playing in an era when many players in the NHL would be considered small by today's standards. His skating, size, and ability to quarterback an offense from the blueline helped the Canadiens to six Stanley Cups. During the Habs' dynasty years in the mid-1970s, in which they won four consecutive Stanley Cups, Robinson also collected two James Norris Memorial Trophies and the Conn Smythe Trophy as the 1978 Stanley Cup playoffs MVP.

Robinson ended his 20-year career as a 10-time All-Star with a record 20 consecutive years playing in the Stanley Cup playoffs, and a then-record 227 career games in the postseason (a record later broken by Hall of Famer Mark Messier). Throughout his career, Robinson racked up 958 points in 1,348 career games. He also added another 144 points in the playoffs to his overall totals.

Following his playing days, the Hall of Famer became a coach and executive, leading the New Jersey Devils behind the bench during the 1999–2000 season and drinking champagne from the Stanley Cup following that year's playoffs. He would win another Stanley Cup with the Devils in 2002–03.

TEAMS

- **MONTREAL CANADIENS**
  (1972–89)
- **LOS ANGELES KINGS**
  (1989–92)

POSITION

D

DEFENSE

Denis Potvin

NEW YORK ISLANDERS (1973–88)

POSITION

D DEFENSE

With the first overall selection in the 1973 NHL Entry Draft, the New York Islanders chose Potvin, a six-foot, 205-pound defenseman that became the cornerstone of their future dynasty. Comparisons between the defenseman and Bobby Orr were inevitable. Both were six feet tall. Both weighed around 200 pounds. Both won the Calder Memorial Trophy. Both won Stanley Cups. Both were bruising, rugged defensemen with offensive prowess and a toughness that opponents were not sure they wanted to tussle with when things got rough. And from the 1967–68 season through 1978–79 season, only two defensemen won the James Norris Memorial Trophy: Orr (1967–75) and Potvin (1976–79). Potvin was inducted into the Hockey Hall of Fame in 1991.

Mark Howe

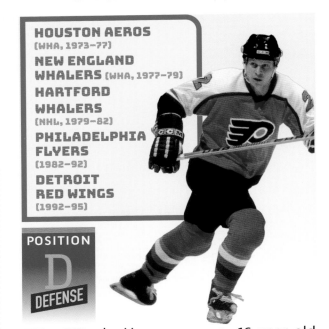

HOUSTON AEROS (WHA, 1973–77)
NEW ENGLAND WHALERS (WHA, 1977–79)
HARTFORD WHALERS (NHL, 1979–82)
PHILADELPHIA FLYERS (1982–92)
DETROIT RED WINGS (1992–95)

POSITION

D DEFENSE

Mark Howe was a 16-year-old junior in high school when he joined the 1972 U.S. Olympic Hockey Team just three weeks before they went to Sapporo, Japan for the XI Winter Olympics. That team unexpectedly struck silver, finishing the Olympic hockey tournament one step below the mighty USSR. Howe's Hall of Fame career spanned 22 seasons, including five years playing on the same line with his brother Marty and legendary father Gordie during their time with the Houston Aeros and New England Whalers. After joining the Philadelphia Flyers, the youngest Howe moved back to the blueline and became one of the NHL's premier defenders throughout the 1980s and '90s. He was inducted into the Hockey Hall of Fame in 2011.

Brian Leetch

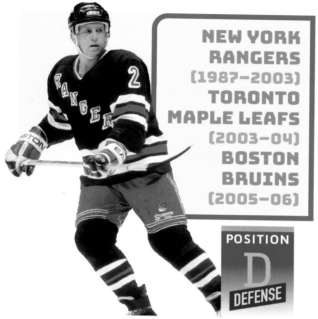

NEW YORK RANGERS (1987–2003)
TORONTO MAPLE LEAFS (2003–04)
BOSTON BRUINS (2005–06)

POSITION
D
DEFENSE

Leetch spent time with three of the Original Six NHL teams but made his name under the bright lights of Broadway in New York City as a member of the Rangers. An integral part of the Rangers' 1994 Stanley Cup victory as the playoffs MVP, Leetch will forever be known as a Ranger. Fellow 1994 Rangers teammate and captain Mark Messier described Leetch as "the greatest Ranger of all-time." Along with a Stanley Cup ring, Leetch's trophy case includes the Conn Smythe Trophy, James Norris Memorial Trophy, Calder Memorial Trophy, and Lester Patrick Trophy. He captained the Rangers from 1997–2000 and was inducted into the Hockey Hall of Fame in 2009.

Victor Hedman

TAMPA BAY LIGHTNING (2009–PRESENT)

POSITION
D
DEFENSE

Standing six foot seven and weighing nearly 250 pounds off the ice, Hedman is an imposing figure. Add pads, skates, and a 103 mph slapshot and you have one of the most intimidating players in today's NHL. The two-time Stanley Cup champion and Conn Smythe Trophy winner is annually considered one of the best defensemen in the league. After the 2017–18 season, he had the hardware to prove it having earned the James Norris Memorial Trophy as the league's top blueliner. A career member of the Tampa Bay Lightning organization, Hedman was the first defensemen in team history to play 1,000 or more games and only the third in team history to hit that mark, behind Vincent Lecavalier and Steven Stamkos.

Goaltenders

The position of goaltender has never been easy. For nearly seven decades of play in the NHL, goalies never wore protective face masks. These unflinching men played the position with bravado, swagger, and toughness. The last line of defense is the truest description of a goaltender's job. Without a great goaltender backing them up, the highest scoring, most potent offense will not be enough to win a championship. Good goaltending is the key to a team's success at any level of play. Period.

> **When I got drafted, I just wanted to play one game in the NHL. I did not really care anything about winning.**
>
> —Martin Brodeur, the NHL's all-time winningest goaltender

Martin Brodeur

FAST FACT:

NHL teams can use emergency goalies. Known as Emergency Back-up Goaltenders (EBUGs), NHL teams all have EBUGs in attendance in the event either team faces a goaltending crisis during the game (injury, illness, or any other unforeseen occurrence). The EBUGs are non-professional and unpaid for their services.

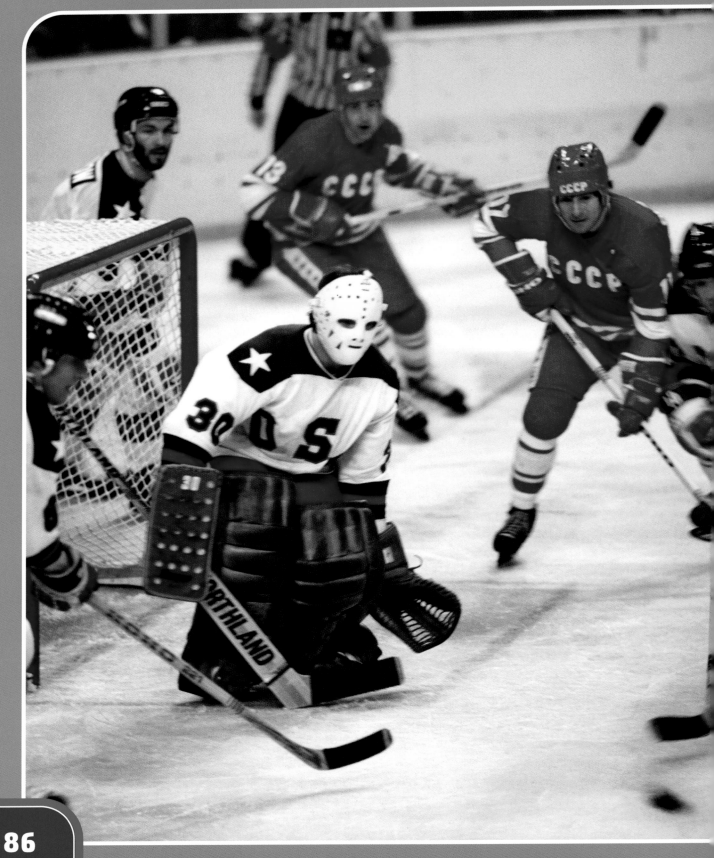

Jim Craig

With the American flag draped around his shoulders after his team won the Olympic gold medal in 1980, U.S. goaltender and hero Craig scanned the crowd in Lake Placid's Olympic Center Ice Rink, desperate to share the gold medal-winning moment with his father.

Two days before, Craig had played the most memorable game in U.S. Olympic hockey history, turning away 36 of 39 shots from the favored Soviet Union team. The Russians had not lost an Olympic hockey game since 1968 and had just beaten the young American squad, 10–3, at Madison Square Garden 13 days earlier.

Despite giving up two goals, Craig's brilliant first period display, featuring 16 saves, along with Mark Johnson's goal with one second remaining in the period, left the teams tied, 2–2. Russian coach Viktor Tikhonov pulled goaltender Vladislav Tretiak after he allowed that last-second goal. Craig continued his stellar play, but the Russians dominated the second period. In the third period, Craig's acrobatics kept his team within striking distance of a win and the Americans ended up in the lead, 4–3, with exactly 10 minutes remaining in the game.

Craig continued his brilliance in the nets, executing a spectacular lunging save with 8:15 remaining and another on a sneaky backhander with just 57 seconds left in the game. As the seconds ticked down, the crowd going wild, the scoreboard finally hit zero and the Americans had beaten the Soviets in what sportscaster Al Michaels described as a "miracle."

After winning the greatest upset in U.S. hockey history two days before, the U.S. team, again led by their goalie, went on to defeat Finland 4–2 and win gold.

TEAMS

- **UNITED STATES OLYMPIC TEAM** (1980)
- **ATLANTA FLAMES** (1980)
- **BOSTON BRUINS** (1980–81)
- **MINNESOTA NORTH STARS** (1983–84)

POSITION

G
GOALIE

87

Vladislav Tretiak

Although he never played a single minute in the NHL, it can be argued by players, fans, and anyone who follows hockey around the world that Tretiak was the greatest goaltender of all time.

Tretiak joined the Red Army team as a 17-year-old and made his debut in the nets for the USSR national team in 1969 at the Izvestia Prize tournament in Finland. By 1972, he was the top goaltender in the Soviet hockey system and led his comrades to a gold medal at the Olympic Winter Games in Sapporo, Japan. Several months later, in what was billed as the "Summit Series," when the Soviet Red Army team played eight "exhibition" games against a group of the greatest NHL stars of the day, Tretiak became a household name in North America.

Tretiak was in the Soviet nets for two more Olympic gold medals in 1976 and 1984 and an Olympic silver medal in 1980. His controversial removal from the nets during the United States' "Miracle on Ice" win against the Soviets in 1980 remained a bitter pill for the proud and decorated goaltender to swallow.

Tretiak was without peers in his 15-year career with the Soviet Red Army team. He retired as a lieutenant colonel and was even drafted by the Montreal Canadiens in 1983 as a sign of international respect and honor. In 1989, he became the first Soviet athlete inducted into the Hockey Hall of Fame. He currently serves as the president of the Ice Hockey Federation of Russia.

TEAM

- SOVIET UNION RED ARMY
(USSR OLYMPIC TEAM)

POSITION

G
GOALIE

WHAT'S THE WORD?

Five-hole

PLACING A SHOT BETWEEN THE GOALIE'S LEGS.

Georges Vezina

MONTREAL CANADIENS (NHA: 1910–17, NHL: 1917–26)

POSITION
G
GOALIE

Vezina is the first NHL player to ever have an award named after him, an award given annually to the NHL's top goaltender. The Vezina Trophy is a memorial to a man who began playing for the Montreal Canadiens before the formation of the NHL and is noted as one of the game's first great goaltenders. Vezina played seven seasons for Montreal in the National Hockey Association (NHA), followed by eight NHL seasons. Vezina played 328 consecutive regular-season games and 39 straight postseason games in goal for the Canadiens, from December 31, 1910, to November 28, 1925, when he collapsed in the crease in the second period during a game due to complications from tuberculosis. He died four months later.

Ken Dryden

MONTREAL CANADIENS (1970–79, SAT OUT 1973–74)

POSITION
G
GOALIE

A three-time All-American goaltender for the Cornell Big Red, Dryden went straight from the Ivy League to the NHL to play for the Montreal Canadiens in the 1971 Stanley Cup playoffs. The Habs won the Cup that year and Dryden won the Conn Smythe Trophy. He then won the Calder Memorial Trophy as the NHL's Rookie of the Year the following season. He went on to a Hall of Fame career, winning six Stanley Cups and five Vezina Trophies in eight years with the Canadiens. He retired in 1979, at age 31, was inducted into the Hockey Hall of Fame in 1983, and later became a member of the Canadian Parliament.

Connor Hellebuyck

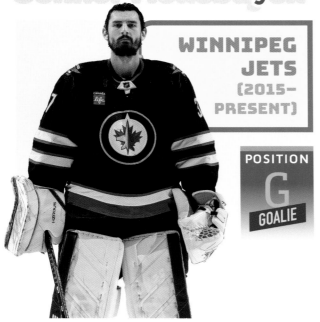

**WINNIPEG JETS
(2015–PRESENT)**

**POSITION
G
GOALIE**

Patrick Roy

**MONTREAL CANADIENS
(1984–96)
COLORADO AVALANCHE
(1996–2003)**

**POSITION
G
GOALIE**

Hellebuyck became just the 23rd goalie in NHL history to win the Vezina Trophy multiple times when he was voted the NHL's top goaltender for the 2023–24 season (he also won the trophy in 2019–20). Hellebuyck was a Vezina Trophy finalist two other times (2018–19 and 2022–23) and has played in four NHL All-Star Games (2018, 2020, 2023, 2024) in just nine seasons with the Jets. Before joining the Jets, he was an All-American goaltender for University of Massachusetts-Lowell and won the inaugural Mike Richter Award as the top goalie in NCAA Division I in 2014.

With 551 wins, four Stanley Cups, three Conn Smythe Trophies, three Vezina Trophies, and being the first goaltender in the history of the game to play more than 1,000 games in the nets, Roy stakes a claim as one of the NHL's all-time greatest goaltenders. During the 2000–01 season, Roy surpassed a once thought to be unbreakable record of 447 wins (set by Terry Sawchuk, 1949–70). That season, he also helped Colorado win the Stanley Cup and won his third Conn Smythe Trophy. Roy retired in 2003 and was promptly inducted into the Hockey Hall of Fame in 2006.

GAME SHORTHAND	Save percentage (SV%): the total saves divided by the total shots faced

Grinders

If we use the word "grinder" in the six states that comprise New England (Connecticut, Maine, Massachusetts, New Hampshire, Rhode Island, and Vermont), it might be confused for a deli sandwich. To those of us familiar with hockey parlance, though, there's no confusion about what a "grinder" is. Also described as "glue guys and gals," "muckers," "sandpaper," and "plumbers," these players do the dirty work needed to make any job successful. Grinders block shots, dig in the corners, agitate, and lots of times in the biggest games, provide the most unforgettable memories.

> *You got to come to work, got to put the work boots on, got to go to the dirty areas, you have got to want to win the puck battle on the wall, you want to take a hit to make a play. That is what it is all about. It comes down to puck battles, offensively, defensively, playing hard and being hard to play against.*
>
> **—Three-time Stanley Cup champion Pat Maroon, on his role with any team he plays for**

Pat Maroon

FAST FACT:

Six brothers—Brent, Brian, Darryl, Duane, Rich and Ron Sutter—from a farm in Alberta, Canada became hockey's first family. From 1976 to 2001, there was at least one Sutter active in the NHL. Collectively, the brothers won eight Stanley Cups, played 4,994 NHL games, and compiled 1,320 goals, 2,934 points, and 7,224 penalty minutes.

Bob Gainey

While helping the Montreal Canadiens win five Stanley Cups in a span of 10 years (1976–86), Gainey became a fan favorite for his grit, determination, speed, and overall play. He also had an admirer from afar. Following the 1979 Stanley Cup Playoffs, Soviet Union head coach Viktor Tikhonov was so impressed by Gainey, he declared him the "world's best all-around player." It was high praise, considering the Russians arguably had some of the world's best players on their own team and were playing games against some of the NHL's very best throughout the mid-1970s and early '80s.

After playing junior hockey in the Ontario Hockey League for his hometown Peterborough Petes, Gainey joined the Montreal Canadiens following their 1973 Stanley Cup win. The Canadiens were on the verge of beginning a run of Stanley Cup victories from 1976–79 and the young left winger was a main cog in the wheel of the emerging dynasty. He was known for his ability to shut down opposing teams' best players. Following the 1977–78 season, the NHL Board of Governors decided to institute a new postseason award for the league's top defensive forward, the Frank J. Selke Trophy. Unsurprisingly and fittingly, Gainey won the trophy in each of the first four years it was awarded.

Gainey's name appeared far less on the scoresheet than some of his superstar teammates, but it was widely understood by experts and close followers of the game that without him, the Montreal Canadiens may not have won as much as they did. However, in the Stanley Cup Playoffs of 1979, Gainey's 16 points and game-winning goal in Game 2 of the Finals sent the Habs to the title. He earned the Conn Smythe Trophy as the Stanley Cup playoffs MVP.

In 1981–82, Gainey became Habs captain, helping younger Canadiens players learn and understand the organization's winning tradition. He was inducted into the Hockey Hall of Fame in 1992.

TEAM

- **MONTREAL CANADIENS**
(1973–89)

POSITION

LW
LEFT WING

Brad Marchand

In his first full season as a Bruin, Marchand ended the 2010–11 season drinking champagne from the Stanley Cup. After 77 games of the regular season in which he scored 21 goals and added 20 assists, Marchand set a Bruins rookie record for playoff goals with 11 in 25 games. In Game 7 of the Stanley Cup Finals, he also began to craft a reputation as a "big game" player when he potted two goals and added one assist in the Bruins' decisive 4–0 win, bringing the Stanley Cup back to Boston for the first time since 1972.

The five-foot-nine, 176-pound winger has built a reputation as an "agitator," the type of player you hate to play against but love to have on your team. His ability to shake the composure of his opponents is what makes his style effective, and he has earned respect around the NHL as a fiery competitor—while also being described by rivals as chirpy, antagonistic, and irritating. Among other names he was called by opponents, he was given the nickname "Little Ball of Hate." Even President Barack Obama asked, "What is up with the nickname?" when the Bruins made their championship visit to the White House.

In September 2023, Marchand's team bestowed their own label on him: captain.

During the 2023–24 playoffs, Marchand joined Bruins legend Ray Bourque as the only other player in team history to record 40 or more multi-point playoff games. He also broke Cam Neely's club record for most goals in the postseason (55). He has played more than 1,000 games for the Bruins, joined six others in the history of the organization to record at least 800 points in a career, and is currently fifth on the Boston Bruins' all-time scoring list.

TEAM

- **BOSTON BRUINS**
  (2009–PRESENT)

POSITION

LW
LEFT WING

GAME SHORTHAND
Penalty Kill (PK)

Claude Lemieux

MONTREAL CANADIENS (1983–90)
NEW JERSEY DEVILS (1990–95; 1999–2000)
COLORADO AVALANCHE (1995–2000)
PHOENIX COYOTES (2000–03)
DALLAS STARS (2003)
SAN JOSE SHARKS (2008–09)

POSITION
RW
RIGHT WING

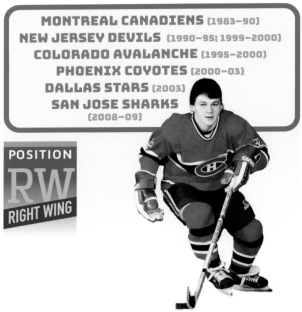

Claude Lemieux was a four-time Stanley Cup champion with three different teams and a clutch playoff performer who won the Conn Smythe Trophy as the Stanley Cup playoffs MVP in 1995. He also epitomized the role of irritant, pest, sandpaper guy, and grinder. His 158 career points in the playoffs, including 19 game-winning goals in 234 games, solidified his reputation as not only a tough opponent to play against but a player who delivered in pressure-filled games. In his final 19 NHL seasons, only once did his team fail to qualify for the playoffs.

Bobby Nystrom

NEW YORK ISLANDERS (1972–86)

POSITION
RW
RIGHT WING

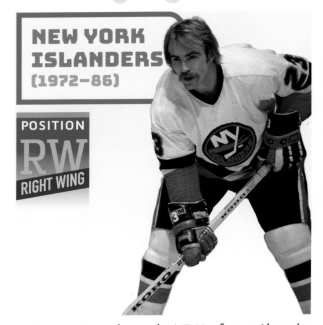

Nystrom's goal at 7:11 of overtime in Game 6 of the 1980 Stanley Cup Finals immortalized him in hockey history and changed his life forever. When he deflected a John Tonelli pass past Philadelphia Flyers goalie Pete Peeters, it led to a hard-fought Stanley Cup victory for the Islanders and marked the beginning of a dynasty on Long Island that would see his team win four consecutive Stanley Cups from 1980–83. Nystrom was not a flashy Hall of Fame, All-Star player, but his clutch goals in the playoffs and during his career exemplified the leadership, hustle, and dedication that made him an Islanders legend.

WHAT'S THE WORD?

Grinder

A TYPE OF PLAYER KNOWN FOR HIS CHECKING ABILITY AND WORK ETHIC, OFTEN ASSOCIATED WITH A PLAYER WHO IS STRONG DEFENSIVELY BUT DOES NOT NECESSARILY SCORE MANY POINTS.

Dale Hunter

QUEBEC NORDIQUES (1984–96)
WASHINGTON CAPITALS (1987–99)
COLORADO AVALANCHE (1999)

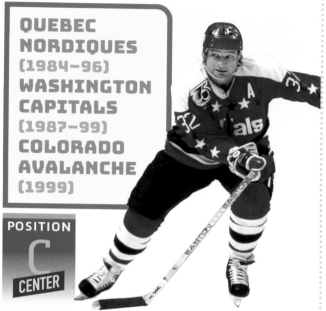

POSITION
C
CENTER

Throughout his 19 seasons in the NHL, Dale Hunter was called many things—agitator, disturber, whiner, gritty, and dirty. But just like any player who would be similarly categorized, he was also a grinder with a penchant to produce in big moments and impose his will to win. The five-foot-nine, 180-pound Hunter never backed down when it came time to get his team started and used any means necessary to win. Along the way, he became the only player in NHL history to score more than 1,000 points (1,020 – 323 goals, 697 assists) and have more than 3,000 penalty minutes (3,565, second all-time to Dave "Tiger" Williams).

Pat Maroon

ANAHEIM DUCKS (2011–16)
EDMONTON OILERS (2015–18)
ST. LOUIS BLUES (2018–19)
TAMPA BAY LIGHTNING (2019–23)
MINNESOTA WILD (2023–24)
BOSTON BRUINS (2024)
CHICAGO BLACKHAWKS (2024–25)

POSITION
LW
LEFT WING

It is an interesting coincidence that many players who are considered grinders find themselves in the Stanley Cup playoffs a lot. For some, like Maroon, fans will also see their names etched on the Stanley Cup multiple times. In Maroon's 16 seasons in the NHL, he has been in the playoffs 10 times. Maroon won the Stanley Cup with his hometown team, St. Louis Blues, in 2019, then went on to win two more in 2020 and 2021 with the Tampa Bay Lightning, making him only the third player in NHL history to win three consecutive Stanley Cups with two teams.

GAME SHORTHAND	Face-off percentage (FO%) The number of face-offs won vs. number of face-offs taken

Wearing the "C"

The captain's "C" on a hockey sweater is a public honor that distinguishes one player on a team from their teammates. Often considered the most talented player on the team, great captains encourage their teammates while also displaying determination, hard work, and grit. Wearing the "C" defines a player's leadership role on the ice, in the locker room, and off the ice. Though not always the loudest voice, most team captains lead by example, and when a team captain does decide to speak, their teammates listen.

> *I started as a fourth-line fighter, went to being a third-line center, then a second-line winger and a first-line center. I have played every role there is, and the only thing that matters is helping the team win.*
>
> **—Six-time Stanley Cup champion Mark Messier**

FAST FACT:

Connor McDavid became the youngest permanent NHL captain in history when the Edmonton Oilers made him captain on October 5, 2016, at the age of 19 years and 266 days.

Mark Messier

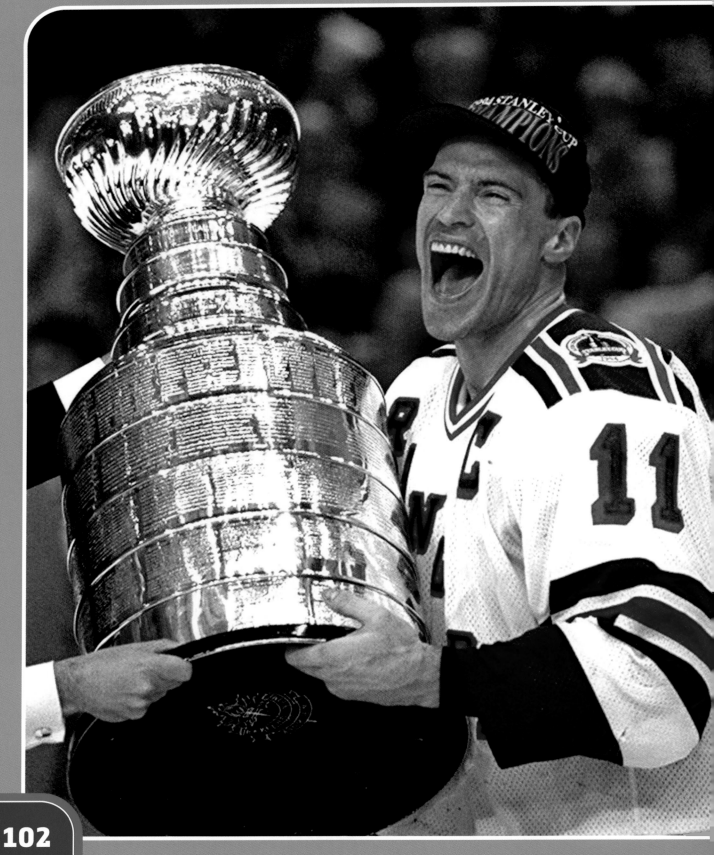

Mark Messier

Known as a one of sports' premier leaders when he arrived in New York in 1991, Messier came to the Rangers with the hope of breaking the organization's Stanley Cup drought, which had stood since 1940. After leading his hometown Edmonton Oilers to five Stanley Cup victories, he wanted to make it six.

In the spring of 1994, with his team down 3–2 to the New Jersey Devils in the Eastern Conference Finals, the confident Rangers captain guaranteed victory for the Broadway Blueshirts in Game 6. Messier proceeded to score three times in the third period of the Rangers' 4–2 win to force a decisive Game 7. His team also won Game 7 and went on to play the Vancouver Canucks for the 1994 Stanley Cup. On June 14, 1994, Messier accepted the Stanley Cup from Commissioner Gary Bettman on behalf of his teammates and all of New York.

Nicknamed "Moose," Messier carried 210 pounds on his six-foot-two frame and possessed lightning speed, intensity, and grit as a newly described "power forward." His size, speed, and intense style of play, along with his power, play-making ability, and goal-scoring skills, would have made him a force in any era of the NHL.

Besides his six Stanley Cups, Messier's trophy case also includes the Conn Smythe Trophy (1984), two Hart Memorial Trophies (1990, 1992), and two Lester B. Pearson Awards—today known as the Ted Lindsay Award (1990, 1992). He was a four-time First Team NHL All-Star and played in the NHL All-Star Game 15 times. He retired as the only player to ever captain two Stanley Cup-winning teams. And on November 13, 2006, the NHL created the Mark Messier NHL Leadership Award, "given to the player who exemplifies great leadership qualities to his team, on-and-off the ice, during the regular season and who plays a leadership role in his community growing the game of hockey."

TEAMS

- EDMONTON OILERS (1979–91)
- NEW YORK RANGERS (1991–97, 2001–04)
- VANCOUVER CANUCKS (1997–2000)

POSITION

C

CENTER

Steve Yzerman

After skating for the Peterborough Petes in the Ontario Hockey League, Yzerman was taken by the Detroit Red Wings with their first pick—fourth overall—in the 1983 NHL Entry Draft. It was the beginning of a professional relationship that lasted 22 seasons in the Motor City, which would include three Stanley Cup championships and countless memories for Red Wings fans.

Eighteen-year-old Yzerman immediately made his presence known in Detroit during his rookie season by setting a Red Wings rookie record with 39 goals. Three years later, at 21 years old, he became the youngest captain ever in NHL history at the time. From 1987 to 1993, Yzerman never failed to register less than 100 points while scoring at least 50 goals five times in that stretch. He also was recognized for his defensive play by winning the Frank J. Selke Trophy in 2000.

For Yzerman, his Detroit teammates, and Red Wings fans, the team's 1997 Stanley Cup win erased a 42-year drought. Yzerman then hoisted Lord Stanley's Cup high above his head a second time following the 1998 playoffs. He also added the Conn Smythe Trophy to his hardware collection.

Yzerman and the Wings added one more Stanley Cup in 2002, but in 2006, the President's Trophy-winning Red Wings were upset in the first round of the Western Conference Quarterfinal. Yzerman also retired that year, after 22 seasons. Shortly after, he assumed the role of Red Wings vice president, and then in October 2008, Yzerman was named executive director of Canada's Olympic hockey team for the 2010 Winter Games in Vancouver. Yzerman helped assemble the team that captured the gold medal for the host country.

Yzerman was inducted into the Hockey Hall of Fame in 2009 and currently serves as the executive vice president and general manager of the Red Wings.

TEAM

• **DETROIT RED WINGS**
(1983–2006)

POSITION

C

CENTER

GAME SHORTHAND	Shorthanded goal (SHG)

Joe Sakic

COLORADO AVALANCHE
(1988–2009)

POSITION
C
CENTER

Traditionally, accepting the Stanley Cup and being the first to hoist it is an honor reserved for the captain of the team that wins it. In 2001, Colorado Avalanche captain Sakic proved his true leadership when he instead passed the prized chalice to teammate Ray Bourque, who had waited 22 years for the moment. Sakic served as his team's captain for 17 of his 20 seasons, making him the second longest serving captain in NHL history (behind Steve Yzerman, 19 years). Through his 20-year career in the NHL, he is one of only a few players to have won the Stanley Cup, an Olympic gold medal (2002), and gold medals in the World Cup of Hockey (2004), World Championships (1994), and World Junior Championships (1988).

Bobby Clarke

PHILADELPHIA FLYERS
(1969–84)

POSITION
C
CENTER

Considered by many to be one of the NHL's all-time great players and leaders, Clarke led the Philadelphia Flyers by example, playing with skill, tenacity, and a fierce determination to win that became the hallmark of his team's Stanley Cup-winning success in the 1970s. In January 1973, the Flyers made the 23-year-old Clarke the youngest captain in NHL history at the time. The young star also became his team's heart and soul, leading the Flyers to back-to-back Stanley Cup titles in 1974 and 1975. In his 15 seasons with Philadelphia, he won three Hart Memorial Trophies as the NHL's MVP and scored 1,210 points (358 goals, 852 assists). He was inducted into the Hockey Hall of Fame in 1987.

Jean Béliveau

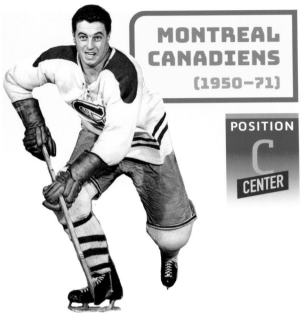

MONTREAL CANADIENS (1950–71)

POSITION C CENTER

In 1961, Béliveau was named captain of the Montreal Canadiens. In 1971, Béliveau's last act as the Canadiens' longest-serving captain (10 years, tied with Saku Koivu) was to hoist the Stanley Cup for the 10th time in his career. That same year, the Canadiens retired his No. 4. When Béliveau retired, he was a 10-time all-star, the leading points scorer in Canadiens history (with 1,219), the fourth player ever to score 500 career goals (507), and the second to score 1,000 points (behind Gordie Howe), as well as the leading goal scorer in Stanley Cup playoffs history (79). In total, his name is on the Stanley Cup 17 times (10 as a player, seven as an executive), an unequalled NHL record.

Jonathan Toews

CHICAGO BLACKHAWKS (2007–23)

POSITION C CENTER

In 2008, Toews was 20 years old and had played 64 NHL games when he was named captain of the Chicago Blackhawks. At the time, no player in NHL history had been named captain earlier. Toews' presence and leadership style of stoic, unwavering commitment to excellence on and off the ice led teammates to give him the nickname "Captain Serious." He led the Blackhawks to Stanley Cup titles in 2010, '13, and '15 in a span of six seasons (2009–15) and became the second-youngest player to win the Conn Smythe Trophy as the Stanley Cup playoffs MVP in 2010. He also won two Olympic gold medals (2010, Vancouver and 2014, Sochi) and the 2016 World Cup of Hockey.

Intimidators

In hockey, when the word "intimidator" is used, it usually means tough individuals. All sports are part physical and part mental. If a team can get its opponent thinking about something other than how they need to play (mental), then the chances of executing a winning game plan (physical) become diminished. While there have been plenty of individual intimidators throughout the years, there also have been teams that seemed to have an advantage before they even stepped on the ice just because of their reputation.

> *This is not only a victory for the Canadiens; it is a victory for hockey. I hope that this era of intimidation and violence that is hurting our national sport is coming to an end. Young people have seen that a team can play electrifying, fascinating hockey while still behaving like gentlemen.*
>
> —Montreal defenseman Serge Savard after his Canadiens team defeated the Philadelphia Flyers in 1976 to win the first of four consecutive Stanley Cups

FAST FACT:

Bobby Hull, Brett Hull's father, was nicknamed the "Golden Jet" for his great skating speed, blazing slap shot, and shocking blond hair while playing most of his Hall of Fame career for the Chicago Blackhawks. His terrorizing slap shot made him one of hockey's most dominant scorers, as he led the NHL in goals seven times in the 1960s and had 13 consecutive seasons with 30 or more goals (including five 50-goal seasons) in 15 years for Chicago.

Serge Savard

The USSR

In September 1972, following a gold medal victory in the Winter Olympics in Sapporo, Japan, earlier in the year, the Soviet Union National Team came to North America to take on the NHL's best in an eight-game exhibition known as the "Summit Series." The NHL players, management, and fans did not think much of the planned games, but the Soviets certainly did. What happened in those now infamous eight games played in North America and Moscow changed the game for future NHL teams and their Soviet counterparts.

Despite losing the overall series, 4–3–1, the Soviets shocked their NHL opponents and fans with their style of play. Their puck control, patience, tic-tac-toe passing, team play, unselfishness, and skating confounded the NHL All-Star Team. The Soviets stunned their NHL opponents, and the Montreal Forum fans, in Game 1 by winning, 7–3. It became very clear after the first game that the North American style of "dump and chase, hit and physically intimidate" was not the only way to win hockey games. The Russians quickly proved their system was an effective alternative to the North American style and that they too could intimidate—without dropping gloves to the ice.

Through the mid-1970s until 1991, Soviet teams, including the famous Red Army team, would travel to NHL cities to take on NHL All-Star teams, as well as the best and most exciting NHL teams of that particular decade. At different times, they played the Montreal Canadiens, Philadelphia Flyers, Boston Bruins, and New York Rangers in front of packed arenas of fans. Ultimately, those games, known as the Super Series, provided exposure to Soviet players who would later be allowed to make their living in the NHL, as well as change the emphasis on a style of play around the NHL and the world.

WHAT'S THE WORD?

Sin-bin

THE PENALTY BOX

Philadelphia Flyers (1974–75)

Having been bounced from the Stanley Cup playoffs in back-to-back years by the St. Louis Blues in the early years of the team's existence, the Flyers were bloodied and broken by the stronger, more physical Blues. Watching the spectacle unfold, Flyers owner Ed Snider vowed his team would never be intimidated again. Management's philosophy moving forward was to create a team that would be physical and uncompromisingly tough. Others in the NHL called it dirty and violent. But the new philosophy worked.

After winning the Stanley Cup in 1975, Philadelphia Flyers goaltender Bernie Parent and captain Clarke, with an iconic and unabashed toothless smile, led their team's victory skate around Buffalo's Memorial Auditorium. Their joy in that moment could not be further from the way in which these "Broad Street Bullies" captured back-to-back Stanley Cup titles.

The hard-charging, grinding, and brawling Philadelphia squad embodied the character of the times and the South Philadelphia neighborhood where they played. The Flyers' nickname foretold what a night playing this tough, rugged, and very talented team would be like. They were first in team penalty minutes during the 1974–75 season, counting up 1,967 minutes, nearly 700 more than the next most penalized team in the league. Along with a potent offense that finished sixth in goals scored and stingy goaltending, some opposing players would suddenly come down with a mysterious, 24-hour case of the "Philadelphia Flu."

Philadelphia made a run for their third consecutive Stanley Cup in 1975–76 but ran into a Montreal Canadiens team—the Flying Frenchmen—that ended the rough and tumble era of the Flyers and changed the definition of intimidation in the NHL.

GAME SHORTHAND

Penalty in minutes (PIM)

Billy Smith

LOS ANGELES KINGS (1971–72)
NEW YORK ISLANDERS (1972–89)

POSITION
G
GOALIE

In an age when taking a run at the goaltender might be part of a team's intimidation strategy, New York Islanders goaltender Smith gave as good as he got. Smith's fiery temper and swinging stick earned him the nickname "Battlin' Billy." During the Islanders' dynastic run of four consecutive Stanley Cups (1980–83), their postseason record was 60–18 and Smith's record in net was 57–13 (wins–losses) in the playoffs. When Smith retired, he left as the NHL's most penalized goaltender in the regular season (490) and playoffs (89), as well as with 305 wins in the regular season and 88 in the playoffs. He was inducted into the Hockey Hall of Fame in 1993.

Scott Stevens

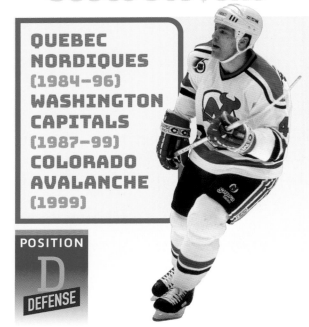

QUEBEC NORDIQUES (1984–96)
WASHINGTON CAPITALS (1987–99)
COLORADO AVALANCHE (1999)

POSITION
D
DEFENSE

A three-time Stanley Cup champion with the New Jersey Devils and winner of the 2000 Conn Smythe Trophy, Stevens combined intimidating defensive skill with offensive prowess to become one of the most fearsome players of his era. When he was on the ice, opposing players kept their heads up and knew where he was at all times—or else. Stevens topped 50 points eight times in his first 12 seasons, including a career-best 78 points (18 goals, 60 assists) with the Devils in 1993–94. That season, he also finished second in voting for the James Norris Memorial Trophy. He ended his Hall of Fame career with 196 goals and 712 assists and was ranked 14th in NHL history with 2,785 penalty minutes.

Cam Neely

VANCOUVER CANUCKS
(1983–86)
BOSTON BRUINS
(1987–96)

POSITION
RW
RIGHT WING

At six foot one and 218 pounds, Neely was a punishing power forward with goal-scorer's hands, which also served him well as a team enforcer when called upon. It was that style that endeared him to Boston Bruins fans for 10 seasons. During that time, he led the Bruins in scoring seven times, including three seasons with 50 or more goals. In 1993–94, he scored 50 goals in 44 games, second fastest to that mark in NHL history (tied with Mario Lemieux) and just behind Wayne Gretzky (39 games). Neely played in 726 regular-season games, racking up 694 points (395 goals, 299 assists) in an injury-plagued 13-year career. He retired in 1996 at age 31 and was inducted into the Hockey Hall of Fame in 2005.

Zdeno Chára

NEW YORK ISLANDERS
(1997–2001 AND 2021–22)
OTTAWA SENATORS
(2001–06)
BOSTON BRUINS
(2006–20)
WASHINGTON CAPITALS
(2020–21)

POSITION
D
DEFENSE

For 24 NHL seasons, six-foot-nine Chára was a towering presence who instilled fear in NHL players. A sure bet Hall of Famer, Chára won the James Norris Memorial Trophy in 2009 and the Mark Messier NHL Leadership Award in 2011 and is the Guinness World Record holder as the tallest player in the history of the NHL. He also set the NHL record for most NHL games played by a defenseman (1,652) and holds the record for hardest shot (108.8 mph, NHL All-Star Skills Competition, 2012). When he captained the Bruins to a Stanley Cup championship in 2010–11, Chára became only the second European-born and -trained player (following Niklas Lidström, Detroit Red Wings) to captain an NHL team to Stanley Cup victory.

United States, Canada, and the World

In the history of hockey, Canada is noted as the inventor of the game. Through the decades, the evolution of players from south of the Canadian border, as well as throughout Europe, Asia, and beyond, has become a noted part of the game. Fans need only look at the various international and world championship events, the Olympic Games, and the rosters of any NHL or major college team to see the far reach and impact the game of hockey has had on the world.

> **All hockey players are bilingual. They know English and profanity.**
>
> **—Hall of Famer Gordie Howe's cheeky nod to one of the core aspects of hockey culture: chirping at opponents during a game**

FAST FACT:

The "Miracle on Ice" game in which the U.S. Olympic Hockey Team defeated the heavily favored USSR Olympic Hockey Team is *Sports Illustrated*'s top sports moment of the twentieth century. In 2008, the International Ice Hockey Federation (IIHF) also recognized that stunning upset as the best international ice hockey story of the past 100 years during the organization's centennial birthday celebration.

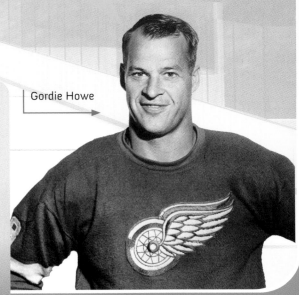

Gordie Howe

Mike Eruzione

If the shot Eruzione took just before the 10-minute mark of the third period on February 22, 1980, versus the mighty Soviet Union at the 1980 Olympic Winter Games had been a few inches to the left, his life might have taken a different turn. The affable captain and U.S. Hockey legend is fond of saying, "Three more inches to the left, and I would be painting bridges for a living."

The final 10 minutes of that iconic game felt like hours to the players, coaches, and fans. But Team USA continued to grind down the Soviets until the final seconds of the game. Eruzione and his teammates—who averaged 22 years old, making them the youngest team in U.S. Hockey history—danced, celebrated, hugged, and could not believe the upset they just pulled off.

Two days later, the U.S. team finished their gold medal dream by scoring three goals in the third period against Finland. Later that day, Eruzione stood on the top step of the medal podium to accept the gold medal on behalf of his teammates and country. As he and his teammates sang the national anthem amid smiles and tears, the reality and magnitude of the moment finally set in. Eruzione called his teammates to the top of the podium and the 20 young men gathered in a group hug.

TEAM

- **UNITED STATES OLYMPIC HOCKEY TEAM** (1980)

POSITION

LW

LEFT WING

FAST FACT:

At the beginning of the 2023–24 NHL season, opening day rosters included players representing 18 birth countries:

Canada—293 (41.4%);
United States—208 (29.4%);
Sweden—64 (9.1%);
Russia—41 (5.8%);
Finland—36 (5.1%);
Czech Republic—23 (3.3%);
Switzerland—10 (1.4%),
Germany—8 (1.1%),
and 10 other countries.

Valeri Kharlamov

In the days of political turmoil amongst Cold War nations, hockey was one area in life that seemed to bring people together, no matter what ideological differences they had. Kharlamov played a big part in helping that thaw take place during his playing career from 1966 to 1981.

Born in Moscow after World War II, Kharlamov was a highly skilled forward who could skate, shoot, pass, and play the game of ice hockey in the highest gear. But he was not well known in North America until 1972, when members of the 1972 U.S. Olympic Hockey Team were some of the first to sing his praises. They saw Kharlamov's talent on the ice firsthand at the XI Olympic Winter Games, where the USSR took home gold.

In Game 1 of the Summit Series in 1972, Kharamov broke open a 2–2 tie with the only two goals of the second period and helped lead the Soviet National Team to a convincing win in the opening game as the game's MVP. After four goals and three assists through the first five games, it became clear to Team Canada players, coaches, and fans that Kharlamov made all the difference. In Game 6, in a vicious display of unsportsmanlike conduct, Philadelphia Flyers captain Bobby Clarke intentionally slashed Kharlamov across the ankle, breaking it and effectively sidelining the Soviet superstar for the rest of the series.

After the series, Kharlamov would continue to dominate Soviet, Olympic, and World Hockey and is today remembered as one of the greatest players in the world. After unfortunately passing away in a car accident in 1981, he was posthumously inducted into the Hockey Hall of Fame in 2005.

TEAM

- **RED ARMY, USSR** (1966–81)

POSITION

LW
LEFT WING

WHAT'S THE WORD?

Twig

A HOCKEY STICK.

THIS TERM DERIVES FROM WHEN THE FIRST HOCKEY STICKS WERE MADE FROM ASH OR HICKORY WOOD. COMPOSITE STICKS, MADE FROM CARBON FIBER AND FIBERGLASS, WERE INTRODUCED IN THE 1990S.

Jaromír Jágr

POSITION
LW
LEFT WING

PITTSBURGH PENGUINS
(1990–2001)
WASHINGTON CAPITALS
(2001–04)
NEW YORK RANGERS
(2004–08)
PHILADELPHIA FLYERS
(2011–12)
DALLAS STARS
(2012–13)
BOSTON BRUINS
(2013)
NEW JERSEY DEVILS
(2013–15)
FLORIDA PANTHERS
(2015–17)
CALGARY FLAMES
(2017–18)

Jágr not only gave NHL fans the thrill of watching him every time he stepped on the ice during his 23-year NHL career, but he also provided a history lesson. The No. 68 that adorned every NHL sweater he wore paid homage to his Czechoslovakian roots and the struggles his family endured during the Communist invasion of his birthplace in 1968. Jágr paid further tribute through his on-ice professionalism and steadfast dedication to the game, his family, and his home country. He finished his career as the NHL's second all-time leading scorer with 1,921 points (766 goals, 1,155 assists), as well as with two Stanley Cup wins, five Art Ross Trophies, three Ted Lindsay Awards, and one Hart Memorial Trophy.

Slava Fetisov

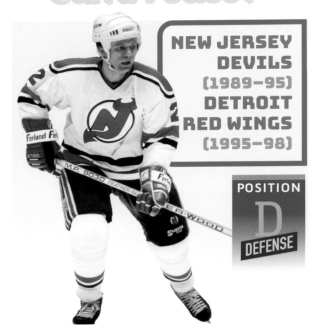

NEW JERSEY DEVILS
(1989–95)
DETROIT RED WINGS
(1995–98)

POSITION
D
DEFENSE

Regarded as one of the greatest defensemen in the world, having led his Soviet Red Army/USSR teams to two Olympic gold medals in 1984 and 1988, as well as multiple World and Soviet Championships, Fetisov ended his NHL playing career in 1998 with 192 assists in 546 games played. But Fetisov's greatest assist may have been the one he passed to future generations of Soviet-born players who dreamed of making a living in the NHL. In 1989, Fetisov asked and was permitted to leave his country to pursue a career in the NHL. Never before had a Communist country allowed one of its premier athletes to willingly—and peacefully—leave. The two-time Stanley Cup champion was inducted into the Hockey Hall of Fame in 2001.

Carter Verhaeghe

TAMPA BAY LIGHTNING (2019–20)
FLORIDA PANTHERS (2020–PRESENT)

POSITION
C
CENTER

Verhaeghe is a young NHL star who has won Stanley Cup championships for both existing Florida-based teams. Originally drafted by his native Toronto Maple Leafs (2013), Verhaeghe was traded twice before ever stepping foot in an NHL arena. He made his NHL debut in 2019–20 and was part of the Tampa Bay Lightning Stanley Cup-winning team that spring. The following season, Verhaeghe left Tampa and traveled south to Miami to join the Panthers. He has enjoyed playoff success in Miami, making two trips to the Stanley Cup Finals and winning the prized trophy in 2024. Along the way, his reputation as a "gamer"—a player that performs well in big games and high-stakes situations—has grown, after scoring five overtime-winning playoff goals in only 17 overtime appearances.

Leon Draisaitl

EDMONTON OILERS (2014–PRESENT)

POSITION
C
CENTER

Edmonton Oilers center and assistant captain Draisaitl is arguably one of the Top 5 players skating in today's NHL. The 28-year-old helped the Oilers come within one win of capturing the 2024 Stanley Cup and has been a force during his 10 years in Edmonton. The Oilers management saw early on that Draisaitl was a special player and signed him to an eight-year contract in 2017. During that time, no one other than teammate Connor McDavid has produced more than Draisaitl. The German superstar ranks second behind McDavid in points (713), posting five 100-plus point seasons, as well as six straight seasons of 30-plus goals including three seasons of 50 or more goals.

13

Sunshine Expansion

On August 9, 1988, the Los Angeles Kings sent shockwaves through the NHL with the acquisition of Wayne Gretzky. While NHL teams had been based in "sunshine states" before (featuring teams like the California Golden Seals, Los Angeles Kings, and Atlanta Flames), Gretzky's move from a hotbed of hockey—Edmonton, Alberta—and away from Canada, the game's nation of origin, opened the floodgates and expanded opportunities for teams from the Atlantic Ocean to the Pacific, including "non-traditional" hockey locales like Arizona, Texas, Florida, North Carolina, Tennessee and, most recently, Nevada.

> **The expansion of the league and the relocation of NHL franchises to fresh precincts have resulted in creating hockey incubators in parts of the United States not normally associated with ice.**
>
> **—Matt Higgins writing for the *New York Times***

Trevor Zegras

FAST FACT:

The NHL expanded in 1967 by adding six new teams: the Los Angeles Kings, Minnesota North Stars, California Golden Seals, Philadelphia Flyers, Pittsburgh Penguins, and St. Louis Blues.

Luc Robitaille

In 1984, Montreal native Mario Lemieux was the talk of the NHL Entry Draft as the No. 1 overall pick by the Pittsburgh Penguins. One hundred and seventy picks later, with the third selection in the ninth round of the draft, the Los Angeles Kings chose their own Montreal native, 18-year-old French-Canadian Robitaille.

Before the draft, Robitaille was regarded as a prospect and not much more. He was a gangly skater who proved himself in the QMJHL. As a member of the Hull Olympiques, he steadily improved until he became a QMJHL First Team All-Star and a standout contributor for Team Canada in the World Junior Championship. He was also named Canadian Major Junior Player of the Year.

Though there was doubt when he arrived in Los Angeles, the six-foot-one, 215-pound winger proved the doubters wrong. Almost immediately, Robitaille scored in the first game of his 1986–87 debut season with the Kings. That season, the left-handed sniper scored 45 goals, added 39 assists, and won the Calder Memorial Trophy as Rookie of the Year. Robitaille scored 53 goals in his sophomore season and went on to average 49 goals per season in his first eight years, including 63 goals in the 1992–93 season.

Trades to Pittsburgh, the New York Rangers, back to Los Angeles, and then to Detroit eventually resulted in Robitaille lifting the Stanley Cup when he played for the Red Wings in 2002. He spent two seasons in the Motor City before returning to the Kings for a final stint. At the time of his retirement following the 2005–06 season, he was the most prolific scoring left winger in the history of the NHL and saw his name at the top of several Kings franchise scoring records. Scoring goals is what made Robitaille a member of the Hockey Hall of Fame when he was inducted in 2009. Currently, he stands at No. 13 on the all-time list of the NHL's best goal scorers.

TEAMS

- **LOS ANGELES KINGS** (1986–94, 1997–2001, 2003–06)
- **PITTSBURGH PENGUINS** (1994–95)
- **NEW YORK RANGERS** (1995–97)
- **DETROIT RED WINGS** (2001–03)

POSITION

LW
LEFT WING

Steven Stamkos

Stamkos had the chance to test the free agent market—to see if other NHL teams might be interested in making him an offer to play for their team—in the summer of 2016. Instead of entertaining other offers, the first overall pick of the Tampa Bay Lightning in the 2008 NHL Entry Draft decided to re-sign an eight-year contract with the Sunshine State-based team.

Through his 16 seasons with the Bolts, Stamkos led Tampa Bay to back-to-back Stanley Cup titles in 2020 and 2021, and the Stanley Cup Finals in 2015 and 2022. As one of the most prolific goal scorers of his era, Stamkos has twice won the Maurice "Rocket" Richard Trophy for leading the NHL regular season in goals scored. In 2023, he became only the 47th player in the history of the NHL to record 500 goals or more and just the 23rd to accomplish that mark with one team.

Stamkos has 214 career power play goals and has recorded double-digit power play goal totals in a season nine times. Since 1996, the Lightning captain is only one of three players (along with Alexander Ovechkin and Auston Matthews) to score at least 60 goals in a season. He potted 60 in 2011–12 and finished second in the Hart Memorial Trophy voting as the league's MVP that season.

He is also a noted leader who has been recognized with the Mark Messier NHL Leadership Award twice in his career. For Bolts fans, no better example of that leadership occurred during the two minutes and 47 seconds he played in Game 3 of the 2020 Stanley Cup Finals. It was his only time on the ice during the series due to injury, but his presence was greatly felt even when he was on the bench. After Game 6, he accepted the Stanley Cup from NHL Commissioner Gary Bettman and proudly skated the prize around the ice before handing it off to his teammates.

TEAMS

- **TAMPA BAY LIGHTNING**
  (2008–24)
- **NASHVILLE PREDATORS**
  (2024–PRESENT)

POSITION

C
CENTER

Marcel Dionne

**DETROIT RED WINGS (1971–75)
LOS ANGELES KINGS (1975–87)
NEW YORK RANGERS (1987–89)**

**POSITION
C
CENTER**

The NHL's sixth all-time leading scorer played the prime of his career in near obscurity after signing with the Los Angeles Kings in 1975. Dionne was drafted second overall in the 1971 NHL Entry Draft by the Detroit Red Wings. Generously listed at five foot nine, the diminutive center from Drummondville, Quebec, hit the ice in his rookie season and proved that size does not matter. Dionne set a rookie scoring record with 77 points during his freshman campaign. Perhaps the greatest player never to win the Stanley Cup, Dionne ended his career in 1989 as the third all-time leading scorer in the history of the game with 1,771 points (731 goals, 1,040 assists). He was inducted into the Hockey Hall of Fame in 1992.

Matthew Tkachuk

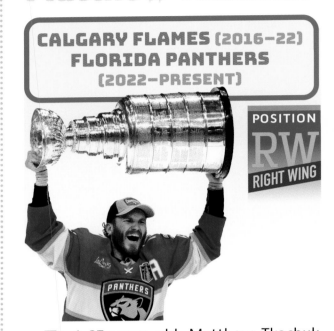

**CALGARY FLAMES (2016–22)
FLORIDA PANTHERS (2022–PRESENT)**

**POSITION
RW
RIGHT WING**

At 27 years old, Matthew Tkachuk can easily say he has been around the NHL his entire life. The son of U.S. Hockey Hall of Famer, 18-year NHL veteran, and five-time All-Star Keith Tkachuk, Matthew Tkachuk grew up in NHL locker rooms and seemed predestined for a career on skates. The nine-year veteran, known for his gritty play, spent his first six seasons in Calgary before being traded to the Florida Panthers prior to the 2022–23 season. Tkachuk immediately became a fan favorite in South Florida, leading the Panthers to the Stanley Cup Finals in 2023. Following the disappointment of losing the final series, Tkachuk came back in 2024 and helped the Panthers win their first-ever Stanley Cup.

Mike Modano

MINNESOTA NORTH STARS/ DALLAS STARS (1989–2010) DETROIT RED WINGS (2010–11)

POSITION C CENTER

Jason Robertson

DALLAS STARS (2019–PRESENT)

POSITION LW LEFT WING

When Modano retired in 2011 after playing 40 games with the Detroit Red Wings, he capped a career unmatched by any U.S.-born player in the NHL at the time. He ended his 21-year, Hall of Fame career as the all-time leading U.S.-born scorer, with a record 561 goals and 1,374 total points, a Stanley Cup ring, and just one game shy of 1,500 NHL games played. Known for his powerful skating and heavy shot (100 mph), Modano spent all but 40 games with the team that drafted him No. 1 in 1988, the Minnesota North Stars/Dallas Stars. He helped bring the Stanley Cup to the Lone Star State in 1999 and a silver medal to Team USA in the 2002 Olympic Winter Games.

The Dallas Stars' 25-year-old left winger is making a name for himself in Dallas and the NHL. Robertson hails from Arcadia, California, and has quietly become a force to be reckoned with, especially during the Stanley Cup playoffs. His 14 goals and 24 assists in 45 career playoff games makes him a noted playoff performer, but his 2021–22 and 2022–23 seasons, in which he scored 41 and 46 goals, respectively, also made him a marked man. Robertson, the lanky-framed, six-foot-three, 202-pound winger of Filipino descent, was the 39th overall draft pick by the Stars in the 2017 NHL Entry Draft. In just a short time, he has proven to be a dependable power play sniper and a rising star in the NHL.

CHAPTER

14

Changing the Game

Not long ago, the faces of hockey were mostly white and male. With the expansion of the game across the U.S. and worldwide, and following the 1972 passage of Title IX civil rights legislation (which prohibited sex-based discrimination in schools or other educational programs receiving federal funding), the game and its players and fans have begun to change noticeably. Today's professional and amateur ranks count Black, Asian, Indigenous, Middle Eastern, and Latinx players, among others, and according to the recent NHL Report on Diversity and Inclusion, six women hold the title Assistant General Manager of their respective clubs.

> *I hope one day I will be able to play in a game in the NHL, not just practice.*
>
> **—Four-time U.S. Women's Hockey Olympian and captain Hilary Knight**

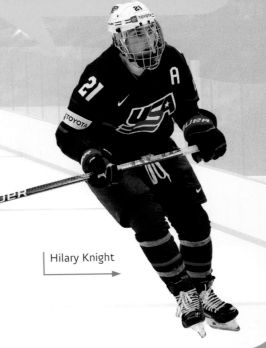

Hilary Knight

FAST FACT:

Dirk Graham was the first Black player to be named team captain when he was given the "C" with the Chicago Blackhawks on January 21, 1989. Nine years later, on June 29, 1998, Graham was named head coach of the Blackhawks, becoming the NHL's first-ever Black head coach.

CHANGEMAKERS
Willie O'Ree

O'Ree became the first Black player in the NHL when he played two games for the Boston Bruins in the 1957–58 season. O'Ree was inducted into the Hockey Hall of Fame despite having played only 45 games in the league because his impact on the sport earned him a spot among other immortals of the game in Toronto.

O'Ree was a talented and productive scorer in junior hockey. Prior to the 1956–57 season, he joined the Boston Bruins affiliate, Quebec Aces, where General Manager Punch Imlach told him what others had been saying for several years before: he had a chance to become the first Black player to make it to the NHL.

Finally, on January 18, 1958, the Bruins summoned O'Ree to join them in Montreal to replace an injured forward in the night's game against the Canadiens, making him the first Black hockey player to lace his skates up and play in an NHL game. O'Ree went on to play 43 games for the Bruins during the 1960–61 season and was then traded to the Montreal Canadiens. Unfortunately, he never again spent time in the NHL. His playing career ended in 1979 as a minor leaguer who endured racial taunts and injustices on and off the ice.

At the time, O'Ree's historic breakthrough was not celebrated as anything special, but he is known as a pioneer. He was recognized with the 2003 Lester Patrick Trophy for contributions to hockey in the United States; inducted into various Halls of Fame, including the Hockey Hall of Fame in 2018; and received the highest honors Canada and the United States can bestow upon a civilian: the Order of Canada in 2008 and the Congressional Gold Medal in 2022, respectively.

In 2018, the NHL honored O'Ree by creating the Willie O'Ree Community Hero Award, presented to the person "who—through the game of hockey—has positively impacted his or her community, culture or society."

TEAM

- **BOSTON BRUINS**
  (1958–61)

POSITION
LW
LEFT WING

135

Grant Fuhr

Fuhr came of age in the NHL as the league was transitioning from an intimidating, rugged style of play to a fast-skating, skillful, wide-open style. He began his Hall of Fame career with his hometown team, the Edmonton Oilers, and spent 10 seasons between the pipes watching teammates Gretzky, Messier, Coffey, Anderson, Lowe, and Kurri change the way the game was played.

Fuhr helped lead the Oilers to five Stanley Cups, won one Vezina Trophy, and was both a constant postseason NHL All-Star and a consummate big-game goaltender. While his career save percentage of .887 and 3.38 goals against average pales in comparison to today's stingy goaltender statistics, Fuhr played in an era when his team was likely to score seven goals and give up six on any given night.

After Edmonton, Fuhr was seen by several teams as a "ray of hope" for more playoff glory and also used as a mentor to rising youngsters in their organizations. But injuries also started to curtail his effectiveness as he embarked on his final seasons. Fittingly, on his return and final trip back to Alberta as a member of the Calgary Flames, Fuhr became the sixth goaltender in NHL history to record 400 career wins when his team defeated the Florida Panthers on October 22, 1999. The milestone win put Fuhr in the company of fellow Hall of Famers Terry Sawchuk, Jacques Plante, Tony Esposito, Glenn Hall, and Patrick Roy in what turned out to be his final season in the NHL.

In 2003, Fuhr's first year of eligibility, he was inducted into the Hockey Hall of Fame.

TEAMS

- **EDMONTON OILERS** (1981–91)
- **TORONTO MAPLE LEAFS** (1991–93)
- **BUFFALO SABRES** (1992–95)
- **LOS ANGELES KINGS** (1994–95)
- **ST. LOUIS BLUES** (1995–99)
- **CALGARY FLAMES** (1999–2000)

POSITION

G

GOALIE

Mike Grier

EDMONTON OILERS
(1996–2002)

WASHINGTON CAPITALS
(2002–04)

BUFFALO SABRES
(2004–06, 2009–11)

SAN JOSE
(2006–09)

POSITION
RW
RIGHT WING

San Jose Sharks General Manager Grier became the NHL's first Black general manager in 2022 after spending 14 seasons as a rugged right winger with four different teams. After playing 1,060 NHL games, Grier ended his playing career in 2011. Upon retiring, he spent time with the New Jersey Devils organization as an NHL pro scout and assistant coach. He then joined his former Boston University teammate Chris Drury in the New York Rangers front office in 2021 as the team's hockey operations coordinator. After working one year with the Rangers, Grier was tapped for his history-making position with the Sharks.

Jarome Iginla

EDMONTON OILERS
(1996–2002)

WASHINGTON CAPITALS
(2002–04)

BUFFALO SABRES
(2004–06, 2009–11)

SAN JOSE
(2006–09)

POSITION
RW
RIGHT WING

Iginla, a no-nonsense player who captained the Calgary Flames to the Stanley Cup Finals in 2004, played in 1,554 NHL games, and compiled 1,300 total points (625 goals, 675 assists) during his 20-year Hall of Fame career. A leader throughout his career, Iginla was a six-time NHL All-Star who registered 30 or more goals for 11 consecutive years and was never afraid to defend himself or teammates when play on the ice got rough. Considered for nearly every individual award the NHL handed out, Iginla won the Art Ross Trophy (2001–02), the Mark Messier NHL Leadership Award (2008–09), and the Ted Lindsay Award (2001-02) and was a two-time winner of the Maurice "Rocket" Richard Trophy (2001–02 and 2003–04).

K'Andre Miller

Miller was the New York Rangers first round pick (22nd overall) in the 2018 NHL Entry Draft. The six-foot-five, 210-pound defenseman has been a mainstay on the New York blueline since joining the Rangers during the 2020–21 season. Though mostly known as a "stay-at-home defenseman" (not known for his offense), on March 19, 2023, Miller became the first defenseman in Rangers' history to record four points in a period with two goals and two assists in the first period of a 7–0 win over Nashville. Miller's amateur career included stints in the U.S. Hockey National Team Development Program, where he represented Team USA twice at the IIHF World Junior Championships, and he was a standout collegiate player for the Wisconsin Badgers.

Henry Boucha

Labeled as one of the most electrifying players in the history of Minnesota hockey, Boucha was a second-round pick (16th overall) in the 1971 NHL Entry Draft, a time when American-born prospects were not highly regarded. A proud member of the Native American Ojibwe tribe, Boucha was a "can't miss" athlete out of high school who was also a skilled football and baseball player. He quickly found a position with the 1970 and '71 U.S. National Team and eventual silver medal–winning 1972 U.S. Olympic Hockey Team. Following the Olympics, Boucha played in six NHL seasons, most notably for the Detroit Red Wings and Minnesota North Stars.

Cammi Granato

In 2010, Granato made history as the first woman inducted into the Hockey Hall of Fame. It wasn't the first time the 15-year Team USA and international hockey superstar was a "first."

During the 1998 Olympic Winter Games in Nagano, Japan, Granato was the first captain of the first U.S. Women's Olympic Ice Hockey Team that won the sport's first gold medal. Following her team's successful tournament, Granato became the first woman hockey player to be voted by all her fellow U.S. Olympians to carry the American flag during the Closing Ceremony.

After having to play on boys' teams while growing up, Granato played for the Providence College women's ice hockey team. Providence won several league titles and Granato was named Freshman Player of the Year and Eastern Collegiate Athletic Conference (ECAC) Women's Hockey Player of the Year. In 93 collegiate games, she scored 135 goals and added 110 assists for 245 points.

Granato went on to earn a master's degree in sports administration from Concordia College and continued to excel on the ice, compiling 178 goals and 148 assists during her 123-game career there. Granato was one of the top female players in the United States and quickly helped establish the U.S. as a formidable opponent to favored Canada at the 1998 Winter Olympics. In six games, she recorded four goals and added four assists as the United States won the gold medal over Canada.

At the end of her international career in 2005, Granato retired as the all-time leading scorer for the U.S. Women's National Team with 186 goals, 157 assists, and 343 points in 205 career games. She received the Lester Patrick Trophy in 2007 for contributions to hockey in the U.S. and was the first woman inducted into the IIHF Hall of Fame (2008), the U.S. Hockey Hall of Fame (2008), and the Hockey Hall of Fame (2010).

In 2019, Granato became the first woman NHL scout, serving with the Seattle Kraken, and three years later was named Assistant General Manager of the Vancouver Canucks.

TEAM

- TEAM USA—WOMEN'S NATIONAL TEAM (1989–2005)

POSITION

C

CENTER

Hayley Wickenheiser

Wickenheiser may be one of the most decorated amateur athletes in the history of Canada. Her collection includes four Olympic Winter Games gold medals and one silver medal, seven World Championship gold medals and six silver medals, awards for being Olympic Tournament MVP in 2002 and 2006, and seven World Championship All-Tournament Team selections, including MVP in 2007.

Wickenheiser collected 18 goals and 33 assists in 26 Olympic games and retired as the all-time leading scorer of the event following the 2014 Games in Sochi, Russia. In 2010, at the Vancouver Olympic Winter Games, Wickenheiser was honored by being asked to recite the Athlete's Oath on behalf of all participating Olympians and carried the Canadian flag during the Opening Ceremony.

Wickenheiser's honors also include nearly 20 years of accolades accumulated in various other amateur and professional women's hockey leagues, including MVP trophies won from the Esso National Women's Championships (Canada), team championships in the Western Women's Hockey League (WWHL), Canadian Women's Hockey League (CWHL), and the Canadian Interuniversity Sports (CIS) Canada West. In 2011, Wickenheiser was named an Officer of the Order of Canada. The Hockey News named her one of the Top 100 Most Influential People in Hockey, and her hometown of Shaunavon, Saskatchewan, named their recreational complex after her: Crescent Point Wickenheiser Centre.

Wickenheiser returned to school to earn a degree in medicine in 2017. The following year, she was named the Assistant Director of Player Development for the Toronto Maple Leafs. Finally, in 2019, Wickenheiser earned her rightful place amongst hockey's immortals with induction into the Hockey Hall of Fame.

TEAM

- **TEAM CANADA— CANADIAN NATIONAL WOMEN'S HOCKEY TEAM**

POSITION

C

CENTER

Angela Ruggiero

TEAM USA—WOMEN'S NATIONAL TEAM (1996–2011)

POSITION
D
DEFENSE

Ruggiero was the youngest member of the first-ever Olympic gold medal-winning U.S. Women's Olympic Hockey team in 1998, where she was a defensive stalwart. She is a four-time Olympic medalist, nine-time member of the U.S. Women's National Team at the IIHF World Women's Championships, and four-time NCAA All-American and Academic All-American at Harvard University, having led the Crimson to the 1999 NCAA Division I Women's National Championship title. When her career concluded in December 2011, she was one of the all-time greatest players in U.S. hockey history. She was inducted into the Hockey Hall of Fame in 2015.

Abby Roque

TEAM USA—WOMEN'S NATIONAL TEAM (2020-PRESENT)

POSITION
C
CENTER

Roque's Olympic debut in 2022 made history the minute she stepped on the ice in Beijing. She was the first-ever Indigenous women's hockey player to represent Team USA. She joined a list of Indigenous players nearly 100 years old that included only three others: Taffy Abel, the first Indigenous player; Henry Boucha; and T. J. Oshie. In seven games during Team USA's silver medal run in 2022, Roque scored one goal and added two assists in her rookie effort. Roque remains a mainstay on Team USA in preparation for the 2026 Olympic Games in Milano Cortina and will be an integral part of her team's potential success.

Marie-Philip Poulin

TEAM CANADA—CANADIAN NATIONAL WOMEN'S HOCKEY TEAM (2007–PRESENT)

POSITION
C
CENTER

This four-time Olympian and four-time medalist (three gold, one silver) is nicknamed "Captain Clutch" for her ability to score in the most important games. The Milano Cortina Olympic Winter Games will be Marie-Philip Poulin's fifth time representing Team Canada. Widely considered the best female player in the world, Poulin always seems to save her best for the Olympic gold-medal games. With two goals in the tournament finale in the 2022 Beijing Olympics, she helped lead Team Canada to the top of the podium for her third time. In total, Poulin has scored in four consecutive gold-medal games at the Olympics, tallying seven goals on the sport's biggest stage.

Alex Carpenter

TEAM USA—WOMEN'S NATIONAL TEAM (2013-PRESENT)

POSITION
C
CENTER

When Alex Carpenter decided to play hockey at Boston College, she skated in the shadow of "The Can't-Miss Kid"—18-year NHL veteran, U.S. Hockey Hall of Famer, and her father, Bobby Carpenter. Though members of the Boston media had long memories of her father, Alex quickly made them forget by carving out a collegiate career that saw her win the 2015 Patty Kazmaier Memorial Award and set career scoring marks at BC in points (267), goals (128), assists (139), game-winning goals (26), power-play goals (25), and shots on goal (820). She also sandwiched in an Olympic silver medal between her sophomore and junior years in 2014 and returned to the Olympic Games in 2022 for another silver medal.

NHL Awards

A wards in any profession represent achievement. In the NHL, awards also represent a long and storied history, as the names of the awards memorialize past great players and founders.

STANLEY CUP
NHL CHAMPIONS

Presented annually to the NHL Champions, the Stanley Cup is the oldest awarded trophy in North American sports. Each winning team members' name is engraved into the trophy.

THE CONN SMYTHE TROPHY
MVP OF STANLEY CUP PLAYOFFS

The Conn Smythe Trophy is presented annually "to the [MVP] for his team in the playoffs" and was first awarded following the 1964–65 Stanley Cup playoffs.

HART MEMORIAL TROPHY
MVP OF REGULAR SEASON

Voted by members of the Professional Hockey Writers Association, the winner of the Hart Memorial Trophy honors "the player adjudged to be most valuable to his team." Established and donated in 1924, was named in honor of former manager-coach of the Montreal Canadiens, Cecil Hart.

TED LINDSAY AWARD

MOST OUTSTANDING PLAYER
AS VOTED BY THE NHL PLAYERS ASSOCIATION

Formerly known as the Lester Pearson Award and first awarded in 1970–71, this award honors the NHL's MVP as voted by the recipient's peers.

JAMES NORRIS MEMORIAL TROPHY

TOP DEFENSEMAN

Named after the former owner of the Detroit Red Wings, the award is presented annually "to the defense player who demonstrates throughout the season the greatest all-round ability in the position."

VEZINA TROPHY

TOP GOALTENDER

One of the NHL's oldest individual awards, the Vezina Trophy was first awarded following the 1926–27 season "to the goaltender adjudged to be the best at his position."

ART ROSS TROPHY

TOP POINT SCORER

Named after Arthur Howey Ross, former manager-coach of the Boston Bruins, and presented to the NHL in 1948, the Art Ross Trophy is presented annually to the player who leads the League in scoring points at the end of the regular season.

MAURICE "ROCKET" RICHARD TROPHY
TOP GOAL SCORER

First presented following the 1998–99 season, the award recognizes the NHL regular season leading goal scorer.

FRANK J. SELKE TROPHY
TOP DEFENSIVE FORWARD

This award honors the NHL forward whose name might not appear on the scoresheet every game but "who best excels in the defensive aspects of the game."

CALDER MEMORIAL TROPHY
ROOKIE OF THE YEAR

This is awarded to the top debut performer in the NHL.

LADY BYNG MEMORIAL TROPHY
SPORTSMANSHIP AND GENTLEMANLY CONDUCT

Another one of the oldest individual awards in the history of the game, the Lady Byng honors the most gentlemanly player and sportsman in the league.

JACK ADAMS AWARD
COACH OF THE YEAR

First awarded following the 1973–74 season, members of the NHL Broadcasters' Association vote for the Jack Adams Award at the conclusion of the regular season to name the coach "adjudged to have contributed the most to his team's success."

LESTER PATRICK TROPHY
OUTSTANDING SERVICE TO HOCKEY IN THE UNITED STATES

Awarded for the first time in 1966, this award honors players, officials, coaches and executives who demonstrate "outstanding service to hockey in the United States."

MARK MESSIER NHL LEADERSHIP AWARD
LEADERSHIP AND GROWING THE GAME

One of the newer NHL individual awards, established in 2006–07, this award is presented annually "to the player who exemplifies great leadership qualities to his team, on and off the ice, during the regular season and who plays a leading role in his community, growing the game of hockey."

WILLIE O'REE COMMUNITY HERO AWARD
IMPACT ON COMMUNITY, CULTURE, AND SOCIETY

The newest NHL individual award was established in 2017–18 season to recognize "an individual who—through the game of hockey—has positively impacted his or her community, culture, or society" in Canada and the United States.

Index

Image Credits

Selected Sources

CHAPTER 2

Arnab Mondal, "What Is a Natural Hat-Trick in NHL? Explaining One of the Rarest Feats in the Game," Sportskeeda, May 15, 2023, https://www.sportskeeda.com/us/nhl/news-what-natural-hat-trick-nhl-explaining-one-rarest-feats-game

"Edmonton Oilers: 1983–84 to 1989–90," Hockey Hall of Fame, https://www.hhof.com/hockeypedia/edmontonoilers_8384_8990.html

"Hockey 101," Cornell Hockey Association, https://www.cornellhockeyassociation.com/hockey/hockey-101/

Tab Bamford, "25 Greatest Hockey Quotes of All Time," The Bleacher Report, March 6, 2012, https://bleacherreport.com/articles/1091621-25-greatest-hockey-quotes-of-all-time

CHAPTER 3

"Americans Selected First Overall," USA Hockey, https://www.usahockey.com/page/show/2603826-americans-selected-first-overall

Hiro Cox, "What Is Hockey Slang for Hair?" Going Hockey. https://www.purehockey.com/c/hockey-hair-go-with-the-flow

"Mario Lemieux Quotes." BrainyQuote. https://www.brainyquote.com/quotes/mario_lemieux_439329

"NHL Statistics Glossary," ESPN, last modified March 12, 2009, https://www.espn.com/nhl/s/statistics/glossary.html

CHAPTER 4

Brad Kurtzberg, "The 20 Most Hilarious Hockey Quotes of All Time," Bleacher Report, December 5, 2012, https://bleacherreport.com/articles/1434502

"Herb Brooks," Team USA, https://www.teamusa.com/hall-of-fame/hall-of-fame-members/herb-brooks

Jacob Messing, "The Ultimate Guide to Hockey Slang," FloHockey, January 18, 2017, https://www.flohockey.tv/articles/5060128-the-ultimate-guide-to-hockey-slang

"NHL Statistics Glossary," ESPN

CHAPTER 5

Andy Kulaszewski, "A Bender's Dictionary: Hockey Slang You May or May Not Know," August 18, 2011, https://bleacherreport.com/articles/810667-a-benders-dictionary-hockey-slang-you-may-or-may-not-know

Michael Russo, "NHL99: Mike Bossy was a goal-scoring machine and a special kind of dad," The Athletic, January 24, 2023, https://www.nytimes.com/athletic/4061594/2023/01/24/nhl-99-mike-bossy/

"NHL Statistics Glossary," ESPN

Player Inductees: Darryl Sittler," Hockey Hall of Fame, https://www.hhof.com/HonouredMembers/MemberDetails.html?type=Player&mem=P198902&list=ByName

CHAPTER 6

Corey Long, "Kucherov becomes 5th player in NHL history to get 100 assists in season," NHL, April 17, 2024, https://www.nhl.com/news/nikita-kucherov-becomes-5th-player-in-nhl-history-to-get-100-assists-in-season

"NHL Statistics Glossary" ESPN

Joe Pelletier, "Adam Oates," Greatest Hockey Legends, https://bruinslegends.blogspot.com/2006/09/adam-oates.html

Messing, "The Ultimate Guide to Hockey Slang"

CHAPTER 7

Adrian Dater, "Ranking the 10 Hardest Slapshots in NHL History," Bleacher Report, November 30, 2016, https://bleacherreport.com/articles/2679131-ranking-the-10-hardest-slap-shots-in-nhl-history

Messing, "The Ultimate Guide to Hockey Slang"

"Montreal Canadiens," Hockey Hall of Fame, https://www.hhof.com/hockeypedia/montrealcanadiens_5556_5960.html

"NHL Statistics Glossary," ESPN

CHAPTER 8

Ankit Kumar, "What is EBUG in Hockey? All You Need to Know about NHL Terminology," Sportskeeda, December 7, 2023, https://www.sportskeeda.com/us/nhl/news-what-ebug-hockey-all-need-know-key-nhl-terminology

"Martin Brodeur Quotes," BrainyQuote, https://www.brainyquote.com/quotes/martin_brodeur_1136953?src=t_nhl

Messing, "The Ultimate Guide to Hockey Slang"

"NHL Statistics Glossary," ESPN

CHAPTER 9

Eugene Helfrick, "The Sutter Family Has Deep Roots in Alberta Hockey," The Hockey Writers, August 19, 2024, https://thehockeywriters.com/sutter-family-alberta-hockey/

Keagan Stiefel, "Playoff Hockey? Bruins Know It's Pat Maroon's Time to Shine," NESN, April 20, 2024, https://nesn.com/2024/04/playoff-hockey-bruins-know-its-pat-maroons-time-to-shine/

NHL Statistics Glossary," ESPN

THW Archives, "How to Talk Like a Hockey Player," The Hockey Writers, April 10, 2024, https://thehockeywriters.com/how-to-talk-like-a-hockey-player/

CHAPTER 10

"Hockey 101: Glossary," NBC Olympics, October 6, 2021, https://www.nbcolympics.com/news/hockey-101-glossary

Joe Pantorno, "Connor McDavid Becomes Youngest Captain in NHL History," Bleacher Report, October 5, 2016, https://bleacherreport.com/articles/2667811-connor-mcdavid-becomes-youngest-captain-in-nhl-history

"Mark Messier Quotes," Quote Fancy, https://quotefancy.com/quote/1324453/Mark-Messier-I-started-as-a-fourth-line-fighter-went-to-being-a-third-line-centre-then-a

"NHL Statistics Glossary," ESPN

CHAPTER 11

Bob Verdi, "Bobby Hull: 100 Greatest NHL Players," NHL, January 1, 2017, https://www.nhl.com/news/topic/nhl-100-greatest-players/bobby-hull-100-greatest-nhl-hockey-players-283864624

Messing, "The Ultimate Guide to Hockey Slang"

"NHL Dynasties: Montreal Canadiens," Hockey Hall of Fame, https://www.hhof.com/hockeypedia/montreal canadiens_7576_7879.html

"NHL Statistics Glossary," ESPN

CHAPTER 12

"7 Interesting Facts about Hockey," WBS Penguins, March 19, 2023, https://www.wbspenguins.com/blog/7-interesting-facts-about-hockey

"Gordie Howe Quotes," BrainyQuote, https://www.brainyquote.com/quotes/gordie_howe_126552

"Hockey 101: Hockey Lingo," Cornell Hockey Association, https://www.cornellhockeyassociation.com/hockey/hockey-101/

NHL Public Relations, "By the Numbers: 2023–24 Opening Day Rosters," NHL, October 10, 2023, https://media.nhl.com/public/news/17309

CHAPTER 13

Cutler Klein, "From Six Teams to 31: History of NHL Expansion," NHL, June 22, 2016, https://www.nhl.com/news/nhl-expansion-history-281005106

Matt Higgins, "N.H.L.'s Warm-Weather Outposts Produce Some Hot Prospects," New York Times, June 23, 2016, https://www.nytimes.com/2016/06/24/sports/hockey/nhl-draft-hot-prospects.html

Messing, "The Ultimate Guide to Hockey Slang"

"NHL Statistics Glossary," ESPN

CHAPTER 14

"Facts, Firsts, and Faux Paus," Hockey Halle of Fame, https://www.hhof.com/thecollection/stanleycup_factsfirstsfauxpaus.html

"Jerome Iginla Quotes," BrainyQuotes, https://www.brainyquote.com/quotes/jarome_iginla_1133075

Mallory Creveling, "Ice Hockey Player, Hilary Knight Talks Body Confidence and Being One of the Boys," Yahoo!Life, October 21, 2014, https://www.yahoo.com/lifestyle/ice-hockey-player-hilary-knight-105353055.html?

Messing, "The Ultimate Guide to Hockey Slang"

"NHL Statistics Glossary," ESPN

NHLPA Staff, "Black Hockey History: A Timeline," NHLPA, February 4, 2021, https://www.nhlpa.com/news/1-22010/black-hockey-history-a-timeline

THW Archives, "How to Talk Like a Hockey Player"

NHL AWARDS

Cody, "The Ultimate Hockey Slang Term Dictionary–146 Essential Hockey Terms," Hockey Topics, October 10, 2023, https://hockeytopics.com/hockey-slang-terms-dictionary/

"Jacques Plante Quotes," BrainyQuote, https://www.brainyquote.com/quotes/jacques_plante_975141

"NHL Statistics Glossary," ESPN

"Trophies," NHL, https://records.nhl.com/awards/trophies

Acknowledgments

With any creative venture, there are always people to thank and acknowledge. With that in mind—whether or not they are aware of the part they played in the creation and writing of this book—we would like to recognize, thank, acknowledge, and shout-out family, friends, colleagues, and others that showed interest or offered counsel, guidance, and encouragement.

Any work we do always starts by acknowledging our parents, the late Barbara and Edward Caraccioli. None of these endeavors would be possible without their guidance and support as positive role models in our lives.

To Kelly, thank you for your constant love and support.

To Mary and Olivia, your guidance, advice, suggestions, and voices are with me forever and serve as a constant reminder of what is most important in life.

Our sister and brothers—Mary Anne Yanos, Rudy Yanos, our late brother Mike Caraccioli, Paul Caraccioli, John Caraccioli, and Kevin Caraccioli—and our in-laws and nieces and nephews all play a part in how we have tried to tell stories. Friends like Greg Osetek, Todd Rucynski, and Murphy and Debra Occhino are as close as family and have our heartfelt love and acknowledgment.

It is a particular thrill for "two hockey obsessed kids from upstate New York," who played on the same Lake Placid ice just a month after the 1980 Olympic hockey team won gold, to have Jim Craig be a part of this book. Thank you for writing the foreword.

Thank you to Lisa Sullivan and Kathryn Waxman from Jim's team at Gold Medal Strategies, Inc.

We also want to thank and acknowledge our team at the Quarto Group— Rage Kindelsperger, Katie McGuire, and Cara Donaldson—who saw value in the idea and let us run with it.

Finally, to all our friends, teammates, hockey parents, extended family, teachers, and mentors who taught, coached, encouraged, and ushered us along the way . . . thank you. Your thoughts, words, and lessons have stayed with us for a lifetime and will never be forgotten.

About the Authors

TOM CARACCIOLI and **JERRY CARACCIOLI** are identical twin brothers and authors of two books, *Boycott: Stolen Dreams of the 1980 Moscow Olympic Games* and regional bestseller *Striking Silver: The Untold Story of America's Forgotten Hockey Team*. Besides co-authoring two books, the brothers also served as editors and advisors for the memoir of Broadcasting and NFL Hall of Famer Lesley Visser, *Sometimes You Have to Cross When It Says Don't Walk*.

The brothers are also contributing writers for *USA Hockey Magazine*, as well as other regional publications. Jerry spent 25 years with CBS Sports and Tom's career spanned 23 years with NBC Sports/USA Network, Turner Sports, and Kroenke Sports & Entertainment/Outdoor Sportsman Group Networks (Outdoor Channel, Sportsman Channel, and World Fishing Network).

JIM CRAIG is best known as the goaltender and backbone of the 1980 Olympic Gold Medal Hockey Team. For more than 30 years, Jim has inspired, instructed, and provided strategic and winning direction to some of the most prestigious companies across the world as the successful owner and president of his company, Gold Medal Strategies, Inc.

To our brother Kevin and friends Mark H., Hack, Louie, Chuckie, Greg O., Wellsy, Dougie, Ahern, PK, Vash, Turtle, Burnsy, Albert, Danny T., Danny F., Morgy, Mike G., Scotty, and others who made playing hockey— in the streets for the "Caraccioli Cup at the Seventh Street Spectrum," and on the ice—a joyous part of our youth, which still continues today when we "lace 'em up."

First published in 2025 by becker&mayer kids!, an imprint of The Quarto Group, 142 West 36th Street, 4th Floor, New York, NY 10018, USA (212) 779-4972 · www.Quarto.com

becker&mayer kids! titles are also available at discount for retail, wholesale, promotional, and bulk purchase. For details, contact the Special Sales Manager by email at specialsales@quarto.com or by mail at The Quarto Group, Attn: Special Sales Manager, 100 Cummings Center Suite 265D, Beverly, MA 01915 USA.

10 9 8 7 6 5 4 3 2 1

ISBN: 978-0-7603-9569-1

Digital edition published in 2025
eISBN: 978-0-7603-9570-7

Group Publisher: Rage Kindelsperger
Creative Director: Laura Drew
Managing Editor: Cara Donaldson
Editor: Katie McGuire
Cover and Interior Design: Foltz Design

Printed in China

Library of Congress Cataloging-in-Publication Data

Names: Caraccioli, Tom, author. | Caraccioli, Jerry, author.
Title: Ice breakers : a kids' guide to hockey and the greatest players who changed the game / Tom Caraccioli and Jerry Caraccioli.
Other titles: Kids' guide to hockey and the greatest players who changed the game
Description: New York, NY : becker&mayer kids!, , an imprint of The Quarto Group, 2025. | Includes bibliographical references and index. | Audience: Ages 8-12 | Audience: Grades 4-6 | Summary: "Written and designed for kids ages 8 to 12, Ice Breakers is a comprehensive look at the great sport of hockey, including everything from notable players both past and present to major historical moments, and more"-- Provided by publisher.
Identifiers: LCCN 2024047538 (print) | LCCN 2024047539 (ebook) | ISBN 9780760395691 (hardcover) | ISBN 9780760395707 (ebook)
Subjects: LCSH: Hockey players--Biography--Juvenile literature. | Hockey Hall of Fame--Juvenile literature. | National Hockey League--Biography--Juvenile literature. | Hockey teams--History--Juvenile literature.
Classification: LCC GV848.5.A1 C37 2025 (print) | LCC GV848.5.A1 (ebook) | DDC 796.962092/2--dc23/eng/20241026
LC record available at https://lccn.loc.gov/2024047538
LC ebook record available at https://lccn.loc.gov/2024047539

Lexile®: NC1370L